Crossroads To Freedom

Sigrid Lehmann Stoesen

NORTH SHORE PRESS
Tampa, Florida

Registered with The Library of Congress
North Shore Press
PO Box 263002
Tampa, Florida 33615

Manufactured in the United States of America
For orders call : Ingram
or Access 1-800-345-0096
or 1-800-507-2665
ISBN 1-891576-07-0
Published by: North Shore Press, Tampa, Fla.
Design and printing by : Pinellas Press

This book is dedicated to my son, Christopher Neal

ACKNOWLEDGMENTS

Warm thanks go to my cousin, Marianne Kuhbier, who was the first to tell me that I should put my experiences on paper; to Susan Conant, who urged me to get my story published; to my sister, Gisela Westermann, and my school friends, Marianne Wagenbach and Ursula Kramer, who shared their experiences with me to add to this book; and to Kurt and Dorit Motyka, who helped me with the history of our hometown. Thanks go to my cousin, Ulrich Koelsche, who refreshed my memory with the history of the Nazi era. I am also grateful to Dr. and Mrs. Heinz Schlicke for their constructive criticism and advice, which I took to heart and made changes accordingly.

My very special thanks go to Dr. Robert Norman, who was instrumental with the publication, and Brenda Fewox and Peter Shea who have given my writing some polish by editing this book. Without these friends my story would still be hidden in a drawer.

Reading Crossroads to Freedom, the reader is brought back to a time when duty and honor, family and tradition came into conflict with totalitarianism and the search for national identity. Sigrid Stoesen's simple story of life during and after the Third Reich reminds us all that no journey through life is ever easy and all situations remain complex, full of meaning and adventure. I highly recommend it for readers of all ages.

Robert Haas PhD.
Dept. of English University of South Florida

Excellent for the student who wishes to understand the most important events of the twentieth century. A remarkable and courageous story of a woman who replaces collective guilt with personal freedom of choice.

Dr. Robert A. Norman
Physician/Author

A fascinating collection of personal memories of a young girl's life and experiences in Germany. Her harrowing journey stretches from Hitler's preparation and declaration of war through Germany's surrender and Communist occupation. The author expresses the emotions of a country and its people with a realization of fear and pain at the disclosure after World War II, and finally celebrates the re-emergence of national pride. Ms. Stoesen describes the Communist's reign, her eventual escape to the U.S., and how she has used her past experiences to carry out her freedom to help others today.
Highly recommended!

Richard Manley
Gaither High School
Social Studies Department

TABLE OF CONTENTS

WORLD WAR II

THE HITLER YOUTH

AIR RAIDS

LIFE IN A CASTLE

ARRIVAL OF AMERICAN TROOPS

TAKE OVER BY RUSSIAN TROOPS

COMMUNISM

HUNGER

NEW HORIZONS - AMERICA

REVOLUTION IN EAST GERMANY

INTRODUCTION

"Crossroads to freedom" is the story of Sigrid, who lived in Eastern Germany during the Second World War, while the whole world around her was turning upside down because of fighting, bombings, destruction and hatred.

It is also the story of Sigrid, who lived as a disillusioned teenager under the communist regime and felt her own world was falling apart.

Sigrid also shared with us her years after the war, when she emerged as an adult from the shadows into a new life in the United States. In that journey she felt the compelling need to help the less fortunate, the disadvantaged, and also felt committed to fight preconceptions of prejudice. Sigrid's life story is an inspiration for the younger generations and a lesson to the elder ones to be responsible for repelling the hatreds by educating young people before the bigotries of their elders have taken root.

There is a deep need for humans, social creatures by nature, to bond together with those whom they feel are most like themselves, as "different" constitutes a threat. Those people who look and talk and move differently than "we" do can't be trusted, we tell ourselves. To many American school children, Germans are perceived as being "different", their past haunted by the crimes of the Nazis. Mrs. Stoesen points out that each human being is deserving the respect, and there are good and not so good people of every kind and variety in every country. It is our responsibility to free our society from bigotry. As Albert Einstein explained: "Human being is part of the whole, called by us the universe. A part limited in time and space. He experiences himself, his thoughts and feelings, as something separate from the rest, a kind of optical delusion of his consciousness. This delusion is a kind of prison for us, restricting us to personal desires and to affection for a few persons nearest to us. Our task must be to free ourselves from this prison by widening our circle of compassion to embrace all living creatures."

Roxana Levin
Foreign Language Professor
Saint Petersburg Junior College

THE SHADOW YEARS

PART I

It was an emotional journey to write down what I have tried to forget, but it helped me deal with the past and left me with the joyous feeling of a survivor.

I invite you to join me on a trip into a time when Hitler reigned in Germany, Communists suppressed us, and a young girl emerged from the shadows into a new life.

Der Nationalsozialismus und das „Dritte Reich" 1933 bis 1945

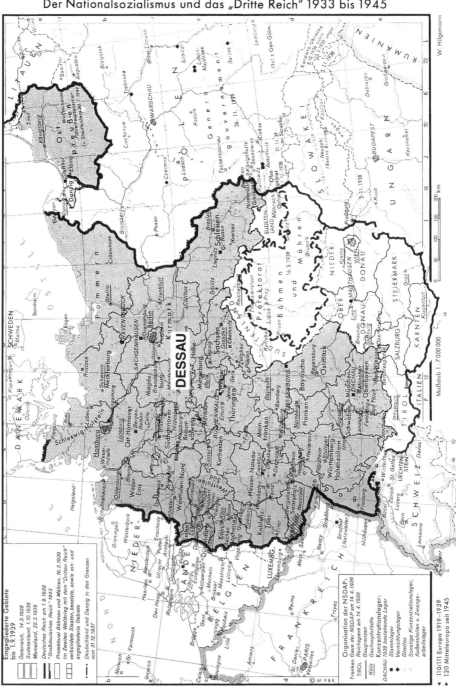

CHAPTER 1

On September 1, 1939, my sister, Gisela, and I were supposed to have a special treat. Mother had planned to take us on a shopping trip to town, which usually meant a stop at a Konditorei (cafe) or a candy store. We could hardly wait to be on our way. To our annoyance we were interrupted by the ringing of the telephone. Mother went to answer it and we were right on her heels, not liking this delay in the least. As Gisela and I waited, we noticed how sad Mother became. Something serious must have happened! Finally Mother broke down and cried. We were highly alarmed; she did not cry easily. "What has happened?" we questioned her anxiously. "Father just called with some devastating news. We are at war!" We were utterly confused. "With whom and why?" were our questions in return. What did this mean for us? She explained to us that German troops had marched into Poland to capture this country in what is now known as the Blitzkrieg (Lightning War).

At 7 and 9 years of age my sister and I knew of wars only from history books, and we asked mother to tell us more about how it would affect us. Of course, nobody could tell us what the future held in store for us. All she could do was tell us about her memories of WWI. Mother had been a young girl during that war and could remember some incidents. What made the most impression on us was that Germans were not allowed to walk on sidewalks by order of the occupying troops, but had to walk in the gutter, and that food was scarce. Her brother died during that war as a German soldier in France; and Westphalia, where she grew up, was occupied by French troops who did not treat the Germans kindly. All this must have been vivid in her mind as she told the two of us about her experiences. We understood war was something terrifying and ugly.

After Hitler came to power in 1933, every young person in Germany from age 10 to 18 was enlisted in the Hitler Youth organization. When I was ten, it was my duty to enroll in the Jungmaedchen (JM) organization, which was part of the League of German Girls or Bund deutscher Maedchen (BDM). JM was a division for younger girls (10-14 yrs.) of the BDM. In one of our Hitler Youth songs we used to sing "Heute hoert uns Deutschland und morgen die ganze Welt" ("Today Germany listens to us - tomorrow the whole world"). This song suggests

Hitler's military ambition to rule the world.

Immediately after war was declared, the stores were empty and ration cards were issued. My father was drafted, along with our car. Our father returned a few days later. He was declared unfit for service because of a hearing problem. Though the army did keep our nice BMW convertible, we were relieved to have our father back home with us.

CHAPTER 2

We lived in Dessau, an industrial town at the Elbe river. Dessau's long history was interesting. In the 16th century, Dessau was a residential town in which the Dukes von Anhalt had their main palace—Schloss Dessau. The principality, and later dukedom von Anhalt, played an important part in the development of Germany. The dukedom reached its peak in the 18th century. Leopold Friedrich Franz von Anhalt, (1740-1817), Vater (Father) Franz as he was affectionately called, was one of the most beloved personalities in the century. He broke with his family's long-time military tradition and devoted his time and efforts to his country's cultural development. Dessau became known for its social reforms in favor of the poor and older population, as well as the development of new forms of education. Most impressive were the designs of the gardens, landscapes and parks. The park of Woerlitz, near Dessau, became a model for parks in the 19th century. It was designed in the English style instead of the customary formal French style of gardens. The English form is based on a natural landscape setting, blending into the surrounding countryside without any fences dividing it. English gardens, while planned, have a natural, spontaneous look to them. Even today visitors flock to see the park of Woerlitz. One site in this park that particularly attracted us as children was a golden urn on a small island. A legend told in our area of the country tells us that the urn housed the ashes of a young princess who was stillborn and had "wished" to be buried there.

The von Anhalts' main palace in Dessau and their other smaller palaces were

Castle Burg Altena

Castle Burg Altena - Entrance to first Youth Hostel in the world

Courtyard Burg Altena

also surrounded by beautiful gardens and parks and were great attractions. Most of the parks were open to the public, and we went for walks in them all the time.

One other famous ancestor of the von Anhalts, the grandfather of Vater Franz, should be mentioned. His name was Leopold I (1676-1747), but is known in history as Der Alte Dessauer (The Old Dessauer). He was a field marshal under Frederick the Great of Prussia and started the military tradition in the Prussian Army to march "in step." His other invention was the "Ladestock" (1718/19), a forerunner of the rifle. He also was a hero in many battles fought for the Prussians.

Another ancestor of the von Anhalts, Catherine the Great of Russia, was a great aunt of the current Duke. Catherine was born Princess Sophia von Anhalt-Zerbst and became one of the most important Empresses Russia ever had.

Beginning in the 19th century, our city was more and more dominated by industry. Junkers, an aircraft manufacturing corporation, had a huge aircraft plant in Dessau where it built the famous JU 52 airplane in 1930. Junkers, therefore, made our city vulnerable to bombing attacks.

Most of my family's friends and neighbors were engineers and pilots. Sometimes a pilot made a nosedive over our house, and the children playing in the yard cheered enthusiastically. Most of our friends and neighbors were not drafted because they were needed to build and test weapons. Thus my sister and I were hardly aware a war was going on and that people in other countries were suffering as German troops advanced.

During the early part of the war my family still went on its usual trips at Easter time to Westphalia, a rural mountainous area in Western Germany, approximately 50 miles from the Dutch border. There, Gisela and I played with cousins and ran wild and carefree in the mountains. We were most impressed by Burg Altena, a very old fortress-castle with a dungeon and watchtowers. One building housed a museum with many artifacts and old armor and weapons, which fascinated us. One basement of another building housed the first youth hostel in the world. It was founded by a good friend of my mother, Richard Schirrmann, in 1909. Today it is a museum with everything furnished the way it used to be. It is so dark and cold, it is hard to imagine how anyone could have stayed there. On the castle complex exists a new youth hostel which looks much more inviting than the old. For me it brings back special memories of the times we visited the founder's sister,

Tante Kaethe. She lived in a tower; and when we came, she let down a long rope with the key so we could let ourselves in. Tante Kaethe called herself the "World Youth Hostel Mother," since she had taken care of the first girls who had come to the hostel. In general youth hostels were there to promote family travel and activities—mainly hiking, rest, recreation and education. The rules were very strict: no smoking, no drinking, and no boys and girls together. And, most important, the hostels were reasonably priced, so everyone could afford to stay there. In 1933, an American Boy Scout leader and an art teacher met with Richard Schirrmann. They were so impressed with the youth hostel program that they began to establish hostels in the U.S.

Westphalia was always my second home. My favorite aunt and cousins lived there, and all my ancestors from my mother's side were born in that region. I always felt as if I belonged, too. That is why it was so relaxing to visit this part of the country.

My parents, sister, and I spent our summers in St. Peter. Now a fashionable resort, at that time St. Peter was only a small rural village at the North Sea. On the farm where we stayed, Gisela and I held the cows' tails while our mother and our maid learned to milk them. We also gathered eggs and played hide and seek in the barns. We rode on top of hay wagons, ran through the pastures and jumped over the ditches that separated the fields (the latter not always successfully). But who cared what we looked like? There was always soap and water! Our whole family, and the friends we took along, spent happy times with farmer Tetens, the owner of the farm.

Look, I've got a new hat!

Just curious

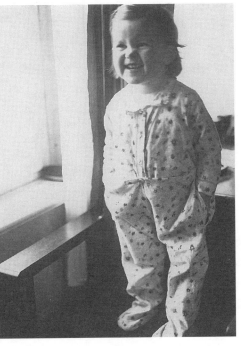

My parent's wake up call

In the park

Having fun

Does the shoe fit?

Through the Dunes of St. Peter / North Sea

Veni
Vidi

Vici

With Mother

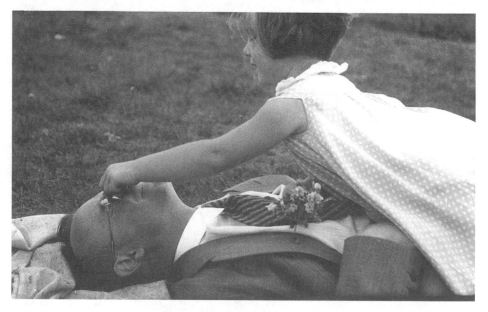

and Father

Gisela and I in Dirndles

The three of us with the farmer's wife
and our maid at the North Sea

Thatched roof farm houses

At the North Sea

First day of school

The "athelete"

In hiding

A country stroll at the North Sea

At the Elbe River with mother

What's happening there?

*Oma Koelsche
(Grandmother)*

Showing off my new purse

Park with wishing temple close to our house

Schloss Dessau
(Left side was our school)

On our usual Sunday walk

Palace in Dessau

Rearview

Mausoleum Dessau
resting place of The Dukes von Anhalt

The Bauhaus (our school) built by Gropius 1925/26

Dessau - Buden, before the bombings...

.....And after.

CHAPTER 3

A lot of my time was devoted to the Hitler Youth movement. Was I ever proud to be a part of it and wear a uniform! Though fabrics became scarce as the war progressed, uniforms were available until almost the end of the war. The uniform was a navy skirt with a white button-down blouse, black neckerchief with a leather slide, and several emblems. For cold weather we wore a tan short jacket and a navy woolen cap with two white front stripes. In later years, the style of the jackets was changed to a more subdued, longer, navy jacket.

We attended meetings twice a week, on Wednesday and Saturday. Sundays were mainly reserved for large gatherings or marches and parades. During our weekly meetings we met in a room like a converted basement, lent to us by a private family. We learned arts and crafts, rolled bandages, and picked herb leaves (mainly from birch trees) for tea. We also collected papers, rags and metal to be used as war materials. Another thing we did was to experiment with making toys (we found numerous ways to make dolls). We knitted pulse warmers for soldiers—short mittens without fingers that just covered the pulse—and sewed baby clothes for mothers in need. People were urged to eat a one-pot meal (like a stew) once a week and give the money saved on the food to an organization that gave aid during the winter to people in need—Winterhilfswerk (WHW). For the same purpose it was required of us to sell little ornaments, like Christmas tree decorations, in the streets or to friends and neighbors. The money was put into a round tin can. The tin was red and decorated with a swastika. Usually I went to my father's company to receive a large donation and, therefore, was spared from the collections in the street. Parts of our meetings were filled with singing, marching through the streets, and talking about current events. On maps, we followed the advancement of our troops in Norway, Denmark, Holland, Belgium, France, and finally, Russia. Hitler was serious about his dream to rule the world, and Germans followed blindly. The Germans were told that "it is their duty to defend the reality of Socialism and its achievements." (Voices from the Third Reich, Regnery Gateway, Washington, D.C., 1989, page xiv.)

From time to time, we had big gatherings on an open field where we demon strated our folk dancing and gymnastic skills. All the girls from Dessau were divided into big circles for the dancing, but each circle had to be in rhythm with the rest. For these dances we were required to be barefoot and wear white mid-calf-length dresses with short vests, which could be any color. For the gymnastic part, we wore black shorts and white, sleeveless T-shirts bearing the black swastika on a red and white background which was sewn to the shirt. We performed with hula hoops, batons, or did floor exercises. It really must have been a pretty picture, and we enjoyed participating in it.

The Hitler Youth often has been compared to the Girl Scouts and Boy Scouts. There are many similarities, to be sure. Boys and girls were separated. Both organizations appeal to young people, and they teach skills that are not taught in school. The Hitler Youth had a ranking system (similar to the Boy and Girl Scouts). Girls with leadership qualities and intelligence were chosen for these positions. After a leader had been in office for a year, she received a cord to wear around her slide. The leader with the lowest rank received a red-white cord, the second rank a green cord and the third highest rank wore a green-white cord. Each rank had command over a certain number of girls, the highest rank having command over the smaller groups. While the Hitler Youth was mandatory and serious trouble could result from ignoring it, the Girl Scouts obviously have a free choice. Here again, our lives were guided by Hitler's rules.

I found that the most tiring thing about the Hitler Youth were the endless marches and parades where hundreds of youth met. The parades were intended to reinforce Nazi thinking by having high ranking Nazi leaders give "inspiring speeches." Sometimes we had to stand for hours without hearing or seeing anything of what was going on. We snapped to attention during the national anthem and had to raise our right arm to shoulder height while singing. Did our arms ever get tired! But resting your arm on the person in front of you was not permitted.

Every time we met someone in the street, we also had to raise the right arm as a greeting and say "Heil Hitler." Some stores had signs on their doors which said, "Kommst Du in diesen Laden rein, so soll Dein Gruss 'Heil Hitler' sein." ("As you enter this store, your greeting should be 'Heil Hitler.'") Looking back on it today, I do not see any sense for this greeting other than reminding people of

In uniform

Before Folk Dance performance with the Jungmaedchen
(Girls Division of Hitleryouth)

the constant presence of a dictator. While this greeting seems odd to modern readers, at that time we did what we were told to do and the way we were supposed to do it. Can you imagine how strange we felt after the war telling people "Good Morning" or "Hello"?

During one of the parades of the Hitler Youth I got into trouble. My girlfriend Helga asked me to go to the restroom with her. To me, this proposal was a welcome diversion from boredom, and we sneaked out of line. Because our regular school had been converted into a veterans' hospital, our school occupied the top floor of Schloss Dessau. The palace was located right in back of the parade ground, so this palace was our destination.

When we arrived, one of the ladies-in-waiting opened the door for us, and while Helga used the restroom, the lady-in-waiting invited me out onto the balcony. The ladies-in-waiting once had the duty to serve their aristocratic ladies in any capacity required; they were not servants but rather companions. In 1940 this custom did not exist any more, and these ladies were old and in retirement and living in the castle. The ladies-in-waiting had been watching the gathering of the Hitler Youth. Helga joined us shortly, and we felt like queens in comfortable palace chairs, reviewing the parade from this spectacular position.

This behavior did not sit well with the leaders of the Hitler Youth. As soon as Helga and I came downstairs, one of the leaders met us and sent us home in shame. We had orders to report to the highest leader of the district the next day. We did not know what to expect. Our misbehavior had created quite a stir, and we had earned punishment. To show everyone that Helga and I were in disgrace, we were not allowed to wear our JM neckerchiefs for a month.

Physical fitness was stressed in the Hitler Youth, as well as in school. Big sporting events on an individual, competitive basis took place at frequent intervals, for which we had to train for weeks. These events were similar to the Olympics and used most of the same sports, but not as many. It was everyone's ambition to earn a sports ribbon for which we had to meet certain requirements. We had to run at a certain speed, jump a certain height and length, throw a heavy ball the size of a baseball a required length, and meet swimming requirements. I was proud that I actually earned the highest ribbon available to my age group.

Gyms in school had excellent equipment. Since coming to the United States, I have not seen anything comparable in American schools. "To be a German girl is not only an honor but a duty as well," we were told; and this, of course, meant that a good German girl kept physically fit. Hitler aspired not only to have an Aryan race, but a healthy one that would create good workers and bear many children for the furtherance of his ideas.

As children, we were in high spirits and wondered why our elders often were so glum. The adults talked in whispers and stopped when we came closer. Now that I am an adult, I know that our elders were simply afraid to voice their opinions in front of us, as many children innocently repeated in school what they heard discussed within the family circle. Once I questioned my father why we did not have a picture of Hitler hanging on the wall as everyone else had. He curtly answered, "We do not have room on our walls for anything like this."

CHAPTER 4

Children in the Hitler Youth in Dessau never dreamed some people did not like Hitler. To the German people Hitler had come as a savior, and nobody looked at him as a dictator that needed to be destroyed.

The treaty of Versailles on June 28, 1919, had ended World War I. Yet the demands by the Allies—the United States, Britain, France and Italy—had forced Germany to accept a heavy burden of reparations; $33 billion had to be paid to the Allies. The army was reduced to 100,000, the manufacture of munitions within Germany was severely limited, and the Rhineland was to be occupied for 15 years. Germany also lost much land; all the colonies in Africa were taken away. Alsace Lorraine went to France, Poznan and most of West Prussia to Poland, Belgium received some border towns, North Schleswig Holstein went to Denmark, part of Silesia went to Poland, and France was given ownership of the coal mines of the Saar basin.

Germany was transformed into a poor country. Help was definitely needed, and Hitler seemed just the person to restore the country. He had charisma and a power of persuasion unequaled by anybody else in German politics. Ironically, the treaty that was supposed to bring peace was so resented in Germany that it contributed to Hitler's rise to power. "National Socialism was not born in Munich (Hitler's beginnings) but in Versailles." (Voices from the Third Reich, Regnery Gateway, Washington, D.C., 1989, page xxvi.)

In an appeal to the German people, Hitler declared that the National Socialist movement was our citizens' last strength, last hope, and only future. Hitler also initiated the first of a series of "four-year plans." He stated that within four years the German farmer's life would be improved, unemployment eliminated, and the economy would blossom. At the end of his speech Hitler announced, "And now, German people, give us four years time and then judge us. If our plan has not succeeded, I swear to you, as I did when I accepted my leadership, that I will leave this office. I did nothing for gain or reward, I only did it for you." (Dokumente des Dritten Reiches, Zentralverlag der NSDAP, Muenchen, 1942, page 22.)

By starting public work projects like the Autobahn, rebuilding industry, and demanding women to stay home to raise their children (therefore giving their jobs to men), Hitler gave six million unemployed people work within four years. He demilitarized the Rhineland, won back the Sudetenland, and incorporated Austria into Germany, all without using any weapons.

We knew that Hitler's idea was for every family to own a small house and a car. The Volkswagen ("the people's car") was created, and many families started making payments toward one, though the majority never received one. The war interfered with the Volkswagen car's production, and money was in short supply. But Hitler started other social programs that were very popular with the German population. He founded Kraft durch Freude (Strength-Through-Joy), which allowed low-income families to take inexpensive vacations. They even chartered ships to foreign countries. The German worker "never had it so good," and it is understandable that they were strong supporters of Hitler, who made all this possible.

Millions of people were attracted to the idea of National Socialism—a worker's party. Hitler really made us believe that he wanted to give the German people a life of prosperity and well-being. With these ideals, he won many followers. Several former SS men (Hitler's elite Nazis—Schutzstaffel) have testified that they joined the SS because they had seen how Hitler had started to improve living conditions in Germany, and they wanted to help him in this effort. They were patriots and idealists. Most did not expect to be exploited for Hitler's evil deeds, such as the use of concentration camps and the killing of innocent people. Once they were members of the SS, they had to stay with the movement or be interned in a concentration camp.

Everyone seemed to be organized during this time. Men usually joined the National Socialist German Workers Party (NSDAP). The men in the Nazi party were called SA men or Brown Shirts because of their uniforms. The only member in our family was an uncle who later was overseer in a Russian work camp. (To make up for the shortage of German workers, Hitler forcibly imported people from Eastern European countries to do the jobs that were necessary.) My uncle loved his job and felt very important. Those were his glory years. And many other men and women who found jobs through their Nazi affiliation gained respect and status under Hitler. This is another way Hitler appealed to the masses, and therefore they were very loyal to him.

Women were not left out. They organized as the Frauenschaft (Women's League). This group met once a week, usually on Thursdays, in different homes. They knitted and sewed for the poor and talked about all kinds of subjects, not necessarily politics. Hitler wanted them to have many children to continue his "Aryan" race. Mothers were honored with the Mother's Cross. A mother with four children received a bronze cross, with six children a silver cross, and with eight or more children she was eligible for a golden cross. My grandmother, who had nine children, was proud of her golden Mother's Cross. (*See cover of book*)

Hitler also knew how to get cheap labor. As soon as girls finished grammar school and turned 14 years old, they had to serve a year of duty—Pflichtjahr,- as it was called. A cousin of mine worked this year for a family with three children where she did all the housework. Her compensation was three Deutschmark (small pocket change), and sometimes a small gift (like a pair of hose). I was spared this year of duty because I went to high school. It was more important for the government that young people continued their education. However, there was also a program for girls over 18 who had finished high school and were too old for the Hitler Youth. A year was to be devoted to the Arbeitsdienst (Labor Service), where heavy manual labor was expected. This service again required that girls and boys wore uniforms. This time the uniforms were brown with funny looking hats. During marches, they carried a clean spade over their shoulders instead of a rifle. Silently I hoped that I would never have to join this organization or even the BDM, which was for older girls. This was getting too political and very serious. For the Arbeitsdienst I would have to leave home and live in close quarters with other girls. I always treasured my privacy and did not know how I could cope with that. Growing up in the city, I could not picture myself working in the fields and doing manual labor. Later I found out that there were easy ways to get out of it; for example, if you had a job and there was no one to replace you. However, I did not know it at that time, and it hung like a sword over my head.

As children, we did not quite understand Hitler's obsession to keep the Germans as a superior Aryan race. You needed to be blond with blue eyes to meet those standards, and this puzzled us since most Germans have fair complexions, but not all are blue-eyed blondes. This meant that Germans were not supposed to marry foreigners, in order to keep the race pure. This also meant no marriage for people who had a history of mental diseases. If someone had told us that Hitler would actually kill people because they did not fit into his pattern, we would not have believed it. From time to time, strange things happened that we were too young and innocent to understand. I remember the morning of the 9th of November, 1938, when we were not allowed to go out, and it was whispered that Jewish stores had been destroyed and looted. Our family and friends were shocked. When we went into town the next day, we saw broken windows and empty stores and asked ourselves, "What crimes did those people commit that anybody would do this to them?" Of course, we never got an answer. I now know that this shocking event is known in history as the Kristallnacht or Crystal Night for the breaking of the glass.

Hitler had control over everything. He even dictated what books we should read and what other cultures we were supposed to embrace. Libraries had book burnings and threw out all volumes written by Marxists, Jews, and other officially disapproved authors. Artists like Kaethe Kolwitz were also banned. I dare not think what treasures were lost to us!

We did enjoy a certain religious freedom. We could go to church whenever and wherever we wanted. All of my friends and I were confirmed in the Lutheran church. A lot more was made of the event of Konfirmation in Germany than in the United States. The Nazis frowned on the church, but I never heard of any steps they took to prevent people from going.

CHAPTER 5

In blissful ignorance of the hardships yet to come, we spent the first years of the war quite content. At all times families in Dessau, as everywhere else, had to be prepared for air raids. We were required to cover our windows with heavy material or cardboard so no light would shine out. Air-raid wardens checked nightly for any light that might have escaped somewhere. Basements were converted into air-raid shelters with heavy wood pilings strengthening the ceiling. In the basement, emergency bunk beds with makeshift straw mattresses were set up in case of prolonged air raids, and sandbags and water buckets were placed everywhere. Gas masks in varying sizes were issued to adults and children. As the war dragged on, children outgrew their gas masks but no replacements were available. In school, students had classes in first aid. We were well prepared.

People driving in cars through the streets had to cover their headlights until only a small slit let some light through. During air raids, people had to drive completely in the dark. Trains arriving at the railroad station were greeted by blue light, and during air raids the platforms were shrouded in complete darkness. People walking through the dark streets identified themselves by attaching phosphorus stickers to their clothing so they would not bump into each other.

Young men were called to arms, and most went willingly. Some were actually excited to have a chance to save and defend the Fatherland. When Hitler started the war in Poland, he had lied to the people and told them that Germans living in Polish territories had been violently persecuted. He went so far as to stage an assault on radio station Gleiwitz by dressing SS officers in Polish uniforms to capture that station. So Germany had to come to the "rescue," of course. Helmut Schmidt, Germany's former chancellor said, "As Germans, we might call World War II the tragedy of our sense of duty. For generations Germans had been far more successfully educated for doing their duty than for exercising individual political and moral judgment"(Voices from the Third Reich, Regnery Gateway, Washington, D.C. 1989, page xii.) Other invasions into foreign countries were explained by the fact that we wanted to repossess the lands taken away from us after WW I and integrate all German-speaking people with the Fatherland.

Once we were at war with the rest of Europe and the Allies, it became necessary to defend Germany. After all, we were told a lot of propaganda, so we became afraid of a takeover. We also became afraid of our enemies and how they would treat us if we lost the war. Posters on public buildings were supposed to inspire us to work or fight for victory. In railroad stations huge signs told us, Raeder muessen rollen fuer den Sieg ("Wheels must roll for victory"), and we added "and the Nazis must march." Across our street in Dessau hung a banner reading Sieg oder bolschewistisches Chaos, ("Victory or Bolshevistic chaos"), dramatizing it with painted red flames. This so frightened me that I had dreams about it and woke up screaming at night, even when I was already in the United States. The Nazis did know how to persuade and goad the people to do what Hitler wanted them to do.

Factory workers had to work longer hours and in multiple shifts because of the shortage of workers. Women came to the rescue and did men's work in factories. At that time women did not usually do men's work, and feminism had not really appeared.

While the men were at war, German women kept the home fires burning. They had to raise children without fathers, feed them on what little food they could find, and deal with air raids. After the war they had to go into the ruins of destroyed buildings as Truemmerfrauen (women of the ruins). With hammers, they had to clean the bricks so they would be smooth and reusable. After the bricks were cleaned, long lines were formed to throw the bricks to the person closest to the street so they would be stacked up and ready for pick up. Germany's survival and reconstruction owed much to the courage and will power of the German women.

Ever so often we had air raids, but nothing happened at that time. The destination of the bombers flying over our city was mainly Berlin, and we just happened to be in the path of it. In one of his speeches, Field Marshal Goering was supposed to have said that if one foreign airplane ever reached Berlin, his name would be Meier. Goering was so convinced of Germany's military power that it was unthinkable to him that any plane could reach Berlin without being shot down.

During the latter part of the war, dreadful stories were passed on to us of the destruction of Hamburg and Berlin, where many people succumbed to a raging inferno. One of the most beautiful and hardest hit cities was Dresden. The fire there was described as the greatest horror of bombing attacks, and it destroyed many historical baroque buildings and sites. We considered this a senseless act of destruction, as there was no industry. I have read that "Dresden remains for many Germans a symbol of the terror that stalked the Reich from above."(Voices from the Third Reich, Regnery Gateway, Washington, D.C., 1989, page 195.) Closer to home the small, medieval town of Zerbst, Catherine the Great of Russia's home-town, was completely demolished. Many of us had stored our valuables there for safety and lost it all.

On a visit to my grandparents and uncle near Leipzig, we experienced the terror of the war close by. I remember standing with my grandfather in the doorway to my uncle's house when we saw a foreign plane approaching. It looked as if it had been shot and was obviously in trouble. We expected it to drop bombs before it crashed, as the planes usually did in a case like this. My grandfather rushed us into the shelter. We barely made it before we heard a bomb hitting close by the basement window where we were sitting. We were very shaken but extremely glad we were not outside.

To prevent the Allies from bombing important sites, like munitions factories, railroad stations or airports, artificial fog was created to cover those places. The effort was successful in covering the targets, but it was poisonous to people, so the fogging was discontinued after a while.

As time went by, our situation became mortally dangerous. Air raids in our area increased to such an extent that children and adults alike grew physically weary of the constant flight for shelter in the basement at night. Loud sirens penetrated our sleep. First as a forewarning of what was to come, and then the second signal urging us to hurry and seek shelter immediately. Before going to bed at night, we laid out our clothes in such a manner that we could quickly slip into them in the dark. Everyone kept a packed suitcase ready to be carried to the shelter. There we sat, waiting for things to happen. Sometimes we heard bombs hitting houses and felt the earth shaking. It was sheer terror to wait for the bombs to hit us. Every so often a designated person had to go and check the attics for fire-bombs. The bombs were described to us as long, narrow sticks and not very heavy, just heavy enough to crash through the roof. But you were not able to hear the impact in the basement; therefore, it took constant checking. Firebombs were used to set fire to the buildings so they would be more visible to the planes carrying the heavy bombs that caused most of the destruction. When firebombs hit, it was necessary to disarm them before they could cause a fire. I have heard of people who picked them up and threw them out of the windows. Usually buckets of sand or water poured over them disarmed them. It was always a relief to find that we had been spared again and could go back to our rooms. As children, we counted the hours. If or when air raids lasted longer than five hours, school was canceled; otherwise, we could go to school one or two hours later, depending on the length of the raid. It seems we were tired all the time.

Towards the end of the war most industry had been destroyed, and the Allies used civilians as their sole targets. Even today I cannot understand why hospitals with the red cross on their roofs and helpless mothers and children had to be destroyed so brutally. Who can condemn people living under a dictatorship? We were not all Nazis simply because we loved our country.

Soldiers on leave from the front lines could not wait to go back into the war. There they could defend themselves. At home they had to sit helplessly in a bunker and wait for the house to topple down on them. It is hard to describe this fear, but it was with us all the time.

Many families lost their homes and found lodging with those who had rooms to spare. Emergency kitchens were set up, and we as young people helped with the serving of the warm meals.

All over the country, food was getting scarce, and hunger became our companion. Women and children searched the woods for mushrooms and berries and grew vegetables in a patch behind the house. Fortunately, I was healthy and looked it; whereas, Gisela was sickly and looked puny. Consequently, whenever my mother secured some goodies like eggs or milk, she gave them to my sister, Gisela. "You are a sensible girl and understand that your sister needs this more than you do," Mother told me. I did not have the courage to tell her how desperately I wanted just a taste of it. Some of the dishes my mother prepared for Gisela I knew only from their looks and the delicious smell they had. Standing in the kitchen door I silently watched her preparing omelets and other meals for my sister. Once, I overheard someone saying that, when you want something very badly, your heart bleeds. So I said to myself, "I bet I'm bloody all over" and looked at my chest, thinking I could detect some signs of blood. This incident is still so vivid in my mind that I remember what I was wearing—a red dress with white polka dots. Some years ago I told my mother of this episode, and she was shocked because she had no idea I was that hungry. She would have given me a bite if I had spoken up.

CHAPTER 6

By the end of 1943, the situation in Germany had deteriorated to a point that the government felt that children would not be safe in Dessau. School classes were then evacuated to the country with their teachers, Gisela's class being one of them. On the sixth of January, 1944, Gisela was taken in by an elderly couple in Sandersleben, which is approximately 25 miles southwest of Dessau. Her school class was sent to a hotel to live, but because of her fragile health, Gisela was given the privilege of staying with the elderly couple. Though Gisela was taken care of and had good food to eat, she had to work hard in the yard, feeding the animals and milking the goats. Once a week she cleaned the house from top to bottom while her foster mother was visiting in the neighborhood.

In the kitchen, Gisela was responsible for washing all the dishes, no matter how many people they had fed. She remembers one time when the Paulings, her foster parents, invited a large group of prisoners of war to their house for a meal. She recalls that there were so many prisoners that the affair had to take place in the back yard. It was a gesture of kindness to the prisoners, because the Paulings' only son was missing in action after the battle of Stalingrad, and they hoped somebody in Russia would do something like this for him if he was still alive. The Paulings cooked the meal, but the serving and cleaning up were again left to Gisela. What a task for an eleven-year-old!

Gisela also was sent on a lot of errands. She used a four- wheel wooden wagon with which she had to pull loads of coal and potatoes up the hill to the Paulings' house. As she explained to me, the loads were so heavy she had to push from the back to get the heavy wagon up the hill. Even when fighter planes flew very low to shoot at people, she had to go on these trips. When she was caught in an open field, she hid behind the wagon. In the village, she ran from doorway to doorway to hide from the planes and save her life.

She often met prisoners from a concentration camp that was located in the center of the village, and she was saddened by their haggard and tired-looking faces, but she had no way to help them. She did not even know the meaning of a concentration camp at that time. She thought they were ordinary prisoners for whom she felt sorry. As children we were never told about the existence of these camps. We picked up words here and there about the KZs, short for Konzentrationslager (concentration camps), as they were called in German. What we heard sounded so sad that we felt compassion for these poor people.

Adults did not dare to talk about the concentration camps. Everyone was afraid of the Nazis. To criticize our government was unthinkable, the consequences too cruel.

In my sister's spare time, she darned socks. It seems she never played. When I questioned her about this, she said she felt she had to earn her keep. When we shook hands with her, we noticed how rough her hands were. "Gisela is being treated like a maid," I heard my parents tell each other. They did not know how close they had come to the truth, and yet she never complained.

While Gisela was unable to help the concentration-camp prisoners, a school friend in Dessau was more daring. Every morning when she walked to school, she saw the prisoners sweep the streets. It was obvious to her that they were hungry, so she took half of her luncheon sandwich and threw it in the gutter. She did not dare to hand it to somebody. In no time at all somebody picked it up. Fortunately, this gesture went unnoticed; otherwise, the Nazis would have punished her severely and the prisoners also.

My father's company, including their families, also was evacuated. Our destination was Ballenstedt on the border of the Harz mountains, approximately 50 miles southwest of Dessau and not very far from where my sister now lived. How refreshing it was to be so close to the forest and mountains! We rejoiced! Finally there was no nearby industry to put us in danger of air raids! We could hike for hours in the peaceful woods, listening to the birds singing and hearing the sounds of our own footsteps.

When we approached our new home, Father led our family up a mountain path through some small woods and showed us a beautiful palace—Schloss Ballenstedt. Of course my father, mother, and I occupied only a few rooms in one wing; but since we had to leave most of our belongings behind, we had only a few suitcases of clothes with us and did not need more space.

We soon found that the view from the palace was breathtaking! On one side were the lush green mountains, on another the plains and fields. To the north was a lake, and to the south was a small town with an avenue leading directly to the gate of the palace courtyard. This gate was always closed though, because everybody used the winding carriage road through the woods. Although the Duke and Duchess von Anhalt and their five children lived in another wing of the palace, we saw them frequently. Up to that time in my life I had not given much thought to royalty. After Hitler's rise to power, the aristocracy played a minor role in Germany and lost most of its power. They mainly governed over their own personal holdings. It was said that the Duke had vast lands in East Prussia over which he was the landlord until the Russians disowned him.

The oldest daughter of the Duke, the Princess Marie Antoinette von Anhalt, known as "Annette" at that time, soon gave me lessons in court etiquette, so I would be presentable and could go everywhere with her. As it later turned out, this was completely unnecessary. The whole family of the Dukes behaved as naturally as anyone else. Annette was my age, 14 years old, and she was happy to have some company. We soon became fast friends. She did not attend a school but had a private tutor, who was not very strict and left her lots of free time. This also left her lonely, as she missed the interaction with others her age. The Duke and Duchess promoted our friendship and called me separately to their salons every so often to hear what Annette and I were up to. They thought I was a steadying influence on the Princess, as she had a tendency to go astray, pursue men, and do things not suitable for a princess. She was proud of her title and thought everyone knew of her existence. Not so. One day she called the Nazi school that was located in the same city she lived in and introduced herself as the Princess von Anhalt and said she wanted to talk to somebody. The student answering the call told her, "And I am the Emperor of China!" and hung up on her. She loved to tell this story.

A theater was part of the castle complex, and Annette and I could go and watch a play whenever we wanted. The center balcony was reserved for the Duke and his family, and we went often since Annette had a crush on one of the actors. We felt important—like true VIPs (which, of course, she was).

The Duke owned a big country estate and a number of small farms, and Annette and I constantly roamed the countryside picking up treats of fruit from farmers here and there. Annette had a beautiful voice, and we sang together as we took our hikes.

The Duke also sent us to his gardens to pick fruit. We were not enthusiastic about it, and one time we decided to lie down under a tree and rest for a while. Annette and I were fast asleep when a booming voice woke us up. The Duke was standing over us with a frown on his face and scolded us severely, reminding us of our duty. We never fell asleep in the gardens again.

I now think that we should have been more conscientious, as by now all teenagers were accustomed to working hard to help the war effort. In Dessau our class had been recruited for work in a cookie factory, where we had to bag cookies. First it was a lot of fun, as we were allowed to eat as many cookies as we liked; but after a few days, we did not want to take another bite. As it is with everything else, your appetite is satiated when you have too much of a good thing.

In Ballenstedt, we worked in a canning plant where we had to stack cans. My friend, Marianne, from Dessau went right along with whatever needed to be done at the factory when she came to visit us. The employees at this plant were mainly women. However, there was one male prisoner of war whom the women teased constantly. He was a Belgian schoolteacher who was very refined and did not much care for the vulgar jokes. It was always a relief to him when he had a chance to work alongside Marianne and me, he told us, because we could have serious and intelligent conversations. We were very touched.

Prisoners of war were generally accepted into the German work force. Sometimes we were a little suspicious and scared to approach them (Hitler's propaganda had taught us to fear all enemies), but mostly they were respected for the jobs they did and the character they displayed. The Duke employed several

Russian prisoners of war, one of them being the coachman that drove us children around in a pony cart. We were left alone with him, so the Duke must have trusted him. As children, we treated him fairly but sometimes teased him. One time he drove us to the Prince's Garden, which was a big walled-in area with lots of fruit trees and a play house, where we all could play inside. We watched what our coachman might do when we were not around. He picked up an apple and took a bite of it. At that moment we made a tremendous racket inside, and from shock he dropped the apple. Only kids could do something so cruel, and today I feel badly about our actions.

Schloss (castle) Ballenstedt with Theater (right)
and park - aerial view

Schloss Ballenstedt

Church on Schloss grounds

Joachim Ernst, Duke von Anhalt

Edda Charlotte, Duchess von Anhalt

View from castle over Schlosspark and fields from where American tanks approached us.

CHAPTER 7

As the Russians advanced in the East, and more and more German cities were destroyed in the West, many German refugees from all directions poured into this small, and once quiet, town of Ballenstedt. Annette and I wanted to help these new arrivals. For this purpose we had a pony cart at our disposal and set out with a coachman to meet the trains, pick up refugees and take them to shelters, mostly large hotels, where emergency beds or mattresses were in readiness. There Annette and I found food for the refugees and took care of their babies by feeding and washing them, so that exhausted mothers found some relief. Our city turned into one big refugee camp, and everywhere people moved together to make more room for new arrivals. Nobody thought of their own personal comfort; we all helped each other.

In Ballenstedt I had to attend a boys' preparatory school, because there was no such school for girls in town. It was customary during this time to keep boys and girls separate once they reached high school, which also included two years of college compared to the American school system. We loved attending school with just girls because we could talk freer and be sillier without the restraint of having to watch out for boys or somebody trying to impress the boys. I was one of only seven girls, three of them from my class in Dessau, which made it a little easier. Boys and male teachers alike detested us girls. If we girls were not up to par or stumbled over some words, our teachers made a laughing stock of us. "Those dumb girls dare to invade our boys' school; and look at them, they cannot keep up with us," one particular teacher complained constantly. The situation was so bad that one girl was threatened with expulsion when she struggled with a boy to get her coat from a rack during an air raid. The teachers thought boys were such innocent lambs! In wintertime, girls proved to be good targets for snowballs—from all directions. The girls and the boys never learned to get along too well with each other, since teachers promoted this "battle of the sexes." Girls gained more respect and were considered equal to boys when we were sent into the fields to help with the harvest.

Not used to hard work, students quickly became exhausted from picking beans, potatoes, and grain that had been left after the machines had done their work. However, we had the satisfaction of knowing that our contribution was valuable. Every little bit counted! Working in the fields was not only hard work but dangerous as well. We worked unprotected in the open fields; and, whenever we heard planes approaching, we had to hide in ditches or haystacks. One time our class observed from our hiding place planes shooting at a train traveling slowly through the valley. We crept closer into our stacks at the sight of it. During our lunch break, our work was rewarded with a good warm stew from the farmer's wife. Never in all my life have I eaten anything that tasted better than these soups! They consisted of meat, white lima beans, potatoes, carrots, and fresh herbs and spices.

Of course, even in Ballenstedt, the Hitler Youth demanded their share of our time. By then I had risen in rank, and I was a leader over approximately 200 younger girls. Because a large number of the girls were refugees, I had trouble locating and contacting them about regular meetings. Meeting rooms for so many girls were hard to find, so we as leaders organized mainly outdoor activities. We organized groups for baby-sitting and sewing at the Nazi school (N.P.E.A. or National Politische Erziehungsanstalt—National Political Training Institute), which was located nearby on another mountain. This Nazi school was a boarding school for boys from 10 - 18 years old (until they finished high school). These boys were selected mainly for their intelligence and were destined for high leadership positions in the Third Reich. This was an enjoyable time, getting to know the young boys who were far away from home and needed big sisters. I became friends with the nurse and helped her to take care of the little boys.

A new weapon, called a Panzerfaust (anti-tank weapon), found its way to the school, and the older cadets were taught how to use it, as they were expected to join in the fighting eventually. To our horror, one weapon backfired and killed a boy trying to shoot it off during a practice session. We dug a grave and buried him under a cover of wildflowers. This was the first time I had ever seen a dead person, and it moved me deeply. Such a tragedy, and it did not accomplish anything!

For a little while that same year I dated one of the older students from the Nazi school. I will never forget my first date. His name was Hans, and we planned to meet on a lake on the school grounds to go ice-skating. I arrived early and skated with the little kids until they shouted in dismay, "Why don't you ever fall down; you are too good for us!" Feeling sorry for them, I managed to take a long turn and let myself sail down with little grace and lay there sprawled out on hands and knees. When I lifted up my face, I looked straight into the grinning face of Hans, who naturally thought me very clumsy. I survived the embarrassment, and we continued to have a nice, though brief, friendship.

Because of the collapse of the Reich and the approaching Allies, the Nazi school was soon dissolved, and the boys sent home to their parents. Some of the students had to stay behind because their home cities were occupied by foreign troops. Hans was one of the boys that had to stay in Ballenstedt. His hometown was already occupied by the Americans. One day I met him in the street downtown. He just came back from a trip on his bicycle through the front lines, where he had met the advancing American troops. When Hans saw me, he called across the street, "Hey, Sigrid, the Americans send their greetings." Hans thus gave us our first sign how close the Americans were.

Hans and a friend of his came to the riding ring at the castle frequently. Annette and I watched and envied them; we wanted to ride, too. Annette constantly tried to persuade the Duke to give his permission, but he was adamant in his refusal. The Duke did not want others to think that the aristocracy had special privileges.

CHAPTER 8

In the meantime, Hitler ruled with an iron fist. The longer the war lasted, the more people became dependent on him to save us from the occupation and conquest by the Allied troops. Some people actually worshipped him at that time. They thought Hitler had raised Germany from the ashes and that he could perform a miracle with the war. We were always told about secret weapons that would let us win the war in the end. However, many became disillusioned when they read the casualty lists and heard the constant wailing of the sirens. Resistance groups existed and were formed by individuals like ministers, professors, mayors, bureaucrats, ranchers, Christians, the suppressed Social Democrats, average citizens, and the nobility. In February, 1943, students in Munich spread leaflets about the truth of his tyranny and called for sabotage in the defense industry. Even, to a certain degree, the military opposed Hitler. Officers had to follow orders that were against their soldierly honor, and they would not stand for it. They discussed, thought, and planned several coups but never came to a clear decision about how to stop Hitler's tyranny. More than 30 attempts were made to assassinate Hitler. However, through acts of fate—and an efficient security system which saw to changes in his schedule —he always escaped.

As opposition increased, wave after wave of arrests occurred. In prisons and camps, those who had defied Hitler waited to be prosecuted.

A group of Army colonels planned a coup with little hope of success. It did not matter to them anymore if they succeeded, their main purpose was to show the world and record for history that the German resistance dared to be brave enough to make an attempt on Hitler's life.

On July 20, 1944, during a daily briefing at Hitler's headquarters in East Prussia, the Wolfsschanze near Rastenburg, Colonel Graf von Stauffenberg planted a bomb under the table at which Hitler stood with his advisers. Colonel von Stauffenberg found an excuse to leave and later saw the explosion. He thought Hitler was dead and flew back to Berlin, where his accomplices waited for the good news. But Hitler was not dead, only slightly injured. (Some of Hitlers advisers, though, were torn apart by the explosion.) Prosecution set in with full force to capture and punish the colonel and his conspirators. There could only be a death sentence for these brave men. Some took their own lives, others were hanged, shot, or executed. Nobody survived. Colonel von Stauffenberg was shot the same day the attempt was made. The following day his wife, uncle, mother, and aunt were taken to the Buchenwald concentration camp. Two nephews were executed. The children were taken to a home that housed the children of resistance members. Occasionally they were told they would also be sent to Buchenwald to be with the rest of their family. Fortunately, those were just warnings. Little was written about the coup in the papers, and I personally heard of it only when I watched a memorial service on television. Soon these brave men, who tried in vain to save the honor of German history, were forgotten. Germans were busy rebuilding the country after the war. Only on July 20, 1994, were the memories of the failed coup revived. The 50th anniversary was celebrated all over Germany. The Wolfsschanze, which is a museum now, was shown on television.

Germans have something to be proud of. Not only did the country produce great poets, philosophers, musicians, and scientists, but they can also be proud of their heroes. When I think of these heroes, I get angry that Germans are mainly known for their crimes under Hitler. Schoolchildren call us beasts or think us mean. Will history ever forgive and forget? Aren't we worth it?

CHAPTER 9

But I digress. Let's go back again to Ballenstedt during the war years.

Bombings everywhere had gradually gotten worse. Sometimes in the distance we could see the sky aflame with red from cities burning around us. In Ballenstedt, we counted our blessings for being relatively safe. Word reached my family that 84% of Dessau, our hometown, was destroyed in one massive bombing attack on March 7, 1945. Nineteen times Dessau had been bombed, but this was the worst. We wondered how many of our friends had survived and if our house was still standing.

My friend, Marianne, and her family suffered through these bombing attacks, and she told me how terribly afraid she was. She almost panicked whenever she heard the air-raid sirens, particularly when there was no power to activate the sirens, and the sirens had to be driven through the streets and cranked by hand. Through loudspeakers, the population was asked to leave the city. Trucks were standing at certain intersections to move the people out of the danger zone. Nobody knew where the refugees would find shelter; living space was scarce everywhere. Families in the country moved in together and were forced to give shelter to refugees. But nobody could tell beforehand which town or village they would be taken to. Marianne told me how she begged her mother to leave because she could not take the danger anymore, but her mother steadfastly refused. Marianne's father was still away at war, and her mother wanted to be there when he came home; otherwise, he would not be able to find his family, and her mother would not risk this.

In cases where the families had to leave for any reason— mainly because their house had been destroyed in bombing attacks—addresses were written on the bricks of houses to tell relatives where they had gone. Many families were separated during this time, and the Red Cross had a monumental task to find people and to reunite families after the turmoil of the war was over.

A legend had been going around in Dessau about a blind and deaf princess. We never found out her name, but she lived in a palace deep in a park surrounded by a big iron fence. No one had ever seen her or any life inside this park, and we did not know if she existed. As children we had often walked through the area outside of this fence and stuck our noses through the fence in hope of detecting some sign of life there. This legend drew us children like a magnet.

In late 1944, after the bombings in Dessau became so bad, the Duke brought the blind and deaf princess to his palace in Ballenstedt. The blind princess remained a mystery. Then one day Annette and I received a summons to visit the mysterious princess. We were supposed to wear our uniforms and tell her all about the Hitler Youth movement. The princess was in her late seventies. She was awe-inspiring, with several ladies-in-waiting around her. The princess touched us so she could "see" us. We had to talk to her through a long hearing horn. She was interested in all we told her, but she did not voice any opinions and was noncommittal about our involvement in the Hitler Youth.

That same spring, the Princess Marie Antoinette was confirmed in the church on the palace grounds. Her confirmation was an occasion for a great celebration. I was invited to this formal affair, and there was an elaborate dinner in their ornate dining hall. A number of her relatives were present. One of them was her aunt, the Princess Marie Auguste, who had been married to the youngest son of the last German Emperor William II (1859 -1941). (In later years, this Princess Marie Auguste adopted Zsa Zsa Gabor's eighth husband, the Prince Frederick, whom Miss Gabor married in 1986.)

The younger guests were invited to dance; dancing had been strictly forbidden during the war. Because our soldiers were fighting serious battles and many had lost their lives, it was considered inappropriate that the civilian population amused themselves. We were a country in deep mourning. I am sure most Germans did not even feel like dancing because of all the tragedies occurring in our country. But we were teenagers and longed for some fun. We wanted to learn how to dance. A relative, who had come to the celebration, the Earl of Solms, taught us how to take our first dance steps. Though this celebration was a joyous occasion, it seemed a farewell to the old way of life as well—and it was.

In the spring of 1945, the Duke von Anhalt wanted to visit his hunting lodge one more time and invited me to come along with his daughter, Annette. From outside, the lodge appeared to be a simple cottage, but inside it had all the comforts you needed. A coachman had driven us to this remote place with a chest full of silver and plenty of food provisions. At the lodge, Annette and I had to do the cooking and housework. I still can see the Duke standing in the kitchen door telling us stories. At night the Duke loaned us some of his pajamas, embroidered with a crown, to sleep in. He believed at the hunting lodge everything ought to be casual. Annette and I examined the lodge's guest book and found that many generals and aristocrats had visited here, but they were all unknown to me. I added my simple name, Sigrid, to it after writing a short poem that Annette and I had dreamed up.

During the daytime we took long walks through the woods and seemed far removed from the real world. At night we sat around the table and talked as we listened to planes flying over us. The Duke mentioned repeatedly how happy he was to be with us. He liked it that we were not talking about fashions and the latest gossip but were just some natural teenagers. The Duke mentioned that it was only a matter of time now before the Americans would reach us, and we did not doubt him. He also told Annette and me about the time he had spent in a concentration camp. Never before had he revealed any details to anyone because he was released only under the condition that he never talk about the KZ's, as the concentration camps were called in German. If he broke his oath, he would be taken back immediately, never to be released again. With the exception of us children, everybody seemed to have known about these camps, but no details about them had been shared. When we later learned of the atrocities, Annette and I could barely believe such horror and tortures had occurred in our country. Over the years, I blocked out the details and cannot write about them. The Duke was fortunate to have survived, though his health was impaired. The Duke had been imprisoned for listening to foreign radio stations, and somebody reported him. He knew the identity of the person who reported him but did not give us any name. He told us he was powerless to do anything about it.

In a newspaper article, I later read that the Duke and Duchess had helped many Jews to escape to America. The Duke's activities seemed to have been widely known, and in Nazi papers his good name was attacked and slandered. This could have been another reason for his incarceration in a KZ.

Doesn't this tell you what kind of a person the Duke was? He was exceptionally brave and compassionate. Today, everybody praises his extraordinary courage. He had the common touch, and everybody could confide in him. From the lowest kitchen maid to the butler—he was revered. But he knew everything that was going on around him and helped out when necessary. He always treated me like a lady. When we drove out in a horse-drawn carriage, his daughter, the princess, had to sit with the coachman, and I sat next to him. His daughter objected to this violently; she wanted to have this honor, but he made it clear that I was their guest and needed to be treated with all respect.

CHAPTER 10

Our worlds were falling apart, both the real world and the world that we sheltered girls had imagined. We knew wars were cruel and brought out the worst in people, and we knew that soldiers acted irrationally. But we now learned from the Duke that our own people imprisoned and exterminated their fellow Germans for no valid reason at all—just because they held different political opinions or were of a different race! This news was unthinkable, and yet, we had to believe it.

Even Hitler began to realize that Germany could not win the war, and he tried to persuade his advisers to implement his "Scorched Earth Policy." This meant destroying all of the German industry, food, medical supplies, all dikes and dams and all bridges, turning everything into ruins, so the enemy would find nothing they could use. Fortunately, his advisers were opposed to this; and this time, Hitler did not get his way. Hitler had no consideration for the German people, and it still greatly upsets me to think how selfish he was; almost inhuman. In the end only bridges were blown up to slow down the advancement of the Allies. His advisers reasoned that if we destroyed everything around us, we would destroy ourselves. We would have to completely rebuild everything, and this would take a long time, leaving many people without work and needed supplies. Hitler also became disillusioned with the German people. As he thought of destroying himself, he was thinking of destroying all Germans because by losing the war we were proven to be weaker than our enemies. We fought valiantly for him at the front lines and at home; everybody gave their best, and to think he did not even appreciate it! To me this proved over and over again that Hitler could not have been sane. Hitler then gave orders to the German people to fight to the end. We imagined fearfully what the end would be like. We were scared. In Ballenstedt we were caught in the middle between two advancing armies. We did not know who would reach us first, the Americans or the Russians. "God, do not let it be the Russians," we prayed. The Russian fighting troops had a reputation for looting and rape. Refugees from the West, where the Americans were advancing, told of more humane treatment. Over the years, we children had listened to much propaganda, and we were afraid of any foreign power.

On a beautiful day in late April 1945, while I was doing volunteer work at the Nazi school, news reached us that the Americans were only a few miles away. Everybody was urged to find a safe place in case of fighting and gunfire. As fast as my legs would carry me I ran home to the palace, where I found everybody carrying their belongings into the basement. The basement in this palace was no ordinary basement; it was more like a deep cavern. All of the residents sat huddled on benches. Bats were hanging from the ceilings above us, and we were waiting for things to happen. Curiosity got the better of me, and I climbed all the way to the palace's top floor where I could see the American tanks advancing through the fields. The tanks looked like toys from this distance, moving on a board of "Tank Battle." As the tanks came closer, they opened fire. As soon as I saw fire in the park on one side of the palace, I rushed back down to safety. In no time at all, the war was over for us. Our town of Ballenstedt had peacefully surrendered. Some people later blamed the Duke for flying a big white flag, which I am not sure he actually did.

Relieved we had survived this far, the palace residents started moving back upstairs to their rooms. While I waited for my parents to arrive with the rest of our belongings, soldiers came searching the rooms. Suddenly, I was confronted by a tall American soldier, and my knees shook for fear. This soldier began asking me questions in English, if we had any guns, munitions, cameras, etc., to which I replied in a shaky voice that we did not have any of those items. His businesslike attitude changed after that, and he asked me with a grin, "What is your name?" I almost panicked, and all I could stutter was, "I don't understand any English." To my relief my parents appeared just then, and my father, in his very broken English, started a long conversation with the soldier. We learned he was from Texas. Whenever I crossed the courtyard from then on, the American soldiers kept pointing at me and saying, "She doesn't understand any English." I still can hear their laughter.

The Americans had German prisoners of war with them, whom they lined up against a wall. The GI's played with their guns in front of these prisoners, pointing their guns at the prisoners every so often, as if the soldiers were going to shoot the prisoners. The air was filled with tension. I could not bear the sight of this any longer. I listened for the sound of a gunshot, which fortunately never came.

The next day, the prisoners were gone, and a tank stood in the middle of the court-yard. The tank had attracted a lot of children, to whom the soldiers were handing out chewing gum- something none of the children had ever seen or even heard of. Parents detested this immediately, and I think chewing gum has never caught on in Europe.

American officers lived in the part of the palace where the Duke and his family lived. They gave the Duke a new car. It was the only car we saw around town besides jeeps and Army trucks. The Duke seemed more relaxed and happier than I had ever seen him. Looking back on this time, it seems as if we were living in a fool's paradise. It was the calm before another storm.

On May 7, 1945, Admiral Karl Doenitz, who had succeeded Hitler, surrendered to the Allies. The war was officially over.

<u>Chapter 11</u>

On July 1, 1945, we woke up to a nightmare. We found ourselves at the mercy of the Russian troops. By agreement between the Western Allies and the Russians, certain parts of the land that the western Allies conquered was given to the Russians in exchange for a share of Berlin. Berlin was divided into four sectors: American, British, French and Russian.

Strange sounds woke us, deep voices singing even stranger songs. The sound of horses' hooves and horse-drawn carriages filled the air. We could not imagine what had happened overnight. Looking out of the window, we noticed the court-yard was deserted. No American soldier was in sight. What had happened? We heard strange voices in a language completely alien to us. It could only be the Russians!

Then we saw and heard them demanding entrance to each room in the palace. Before they reached us, somebody came with the warning to open doors immediately, as the Russians had shot through locks in several apartments and were ill-tempered if they found locked doors. When they came to us, they silently inspected everything and left.

This time, no soldiers were stationed inside the castle; but when we finally dared to leave the building, we saw Russian soldiers camping in the woods all around us. During daytime, they were all over the houses looking for girls. At night, they came back after them and raped them. The air was filled with the screams of women. In the morning the victims were spotted with swollen and bruised faces. The palace was completely filled with refugees by this time, so the Russian soldiers had a lot of victims to choose from.

Every time we heard footsteps in front of our door, I was pushed into a secret closet with a concealed door, which my family had only discovered by accident. This was not the safest hiding place either, since it could only be opened from the outside. If anything should have happened to my parents, nobody would have known where to find me. I would just have perished. If I happened to be playing with my friend, Annette, servants pushed big wardrobes in front of the door, so it would not be visible. It was amazing how many hiding places we found. Sometimes, coming home, somebody would snatch me into their apartment and hide me as they had just seen soldiers go to our apartment.

Not only the screams filled the night air. Soldiers sang the everlasting Russian melodies, sitting around open fires at night and drinking. We had a good view from our windows to observe all the activity. Though we dressed in baggy pants and jackets, had pigtails, and looked most unattractive, girls were constantly observed going up and down the hill. Our parents feared for us. I still don't know how we escaped!

Several other young girls lived on our side of the palace, and arrangements were made for the group of us to sleep in a different house each night in the city. As soon as it got dark, we took a pillow and blanket under our arms and walked through the woods and down the hill with soldiers sneering after us, "Here they go again, sleeping somewhere else." They knew quite well why we had to do this. I cannot recall how many houses I slept in, but it was always on a hard floor. Sometimes soldiers came to those houses during the night, and we climbed out of the windows to hide in bushes. But we had been safe again for another night!

An endless stream of horse-drawn wagons loaded with army goods and the belongings of the soldiers traveled along the main road along the Harz mountains toward cities further south. Men and women soldiers lay sprawled on top of the wagons, some of them sleeping soundly.

We had never seen a sight like this. Only once in a while did we see trucks, and those were obviously American made.

The question that was foremost in our minds was how an underdeveloped country with little technical and scientific knowledge could have conquered Germany with Germany's sophisticated weapons. Almost until the end, some people believed our secret weapons like the V2 rocket would help us to win the war. It had to be because of the Allies' overwhelming manpower. Germany was just a small country compared to the world powers conquering us.

We all grew numb from lack of sleep, lack of food, lack of fresh air, and lack of freedom to move around as we were used to. I cannot recall much of the next few months except that we were constantly in fear. It was an existence, not a life.

One conversation with the Duke stays forever in my mind. We discussed the situation in which we were in and, particularly, his precarious position. He revealed that the Americans had offered to take him, with his family and all their belongings, to West Germany before the Russians came. He had refused, because he said he wanted to die where his ancestors had lived and died for centuries. It was obvious he was resigned to his fate.

CHAPTER 12

Finally, in September, 1945, we were allowed to move back to our hometown. Our house was still standing, and the windows that had been broken in air raids had been replaced. Before moving to the mountains, we had taken all of our valuables, including paintings, silver, and furniture, to friends in small towns where we thought it would be safe from bombs. Ironically, everything was lost in air raids there, while at home nothing had been touched.

Since so many people were homeless, space per person was measured in square meter, and everything one had in excess of the authorized limits would be given to another family. We had to take in a mother and her grown daughter. Our neighbors had to take in a Russian colonel. Many Russians had quarters with German families, and a whole district close by had to be vacated for Russian families. The district was surrounded by a fence, so no Germans had access to it. The Russian soldiers were under better control in the city, and our nights became more peaceful. Of course, things happened when people went out; their watches or jewelry would be taken from them.

It was not uncommon to find a soldier with watches lined up from wrist to elbow. Also in popular demand were bicycles.

Germany was an attractive country for the Russians, and many of them had not been exposed to much culture. The story went that Russian women washed vegetables in toilet bowls, until they were instructed what to do with them. My favorite story is how Russian soldiers liked Germany because "every time you push a button, a woman comes out." This meant every time they rang a doorbell, a woman answered the door.

Officially, our part of the country had become the German Democratic Republic (DDR) of East Germany and was ruled by Communists. A great tragedy and disappointment was the behavior of some German people. A number of them could hardly wait to come into good graces with the new communist government and told on their neighbors and friends. Almost every day we heard of somebody else who had been imprisoned for saying something "unsuitable" that was taken for anti-Communism. People vanished overnight. We were old and smart enough by then to watch our tongues. We could not trust anybody.

Originally, the SPD (Social Democratic Party) was stronger than the KPD (Communist Party); however, the KPD forced the SPD to merge with them to form the SED (Social Unity Party), in which of course the Communists ruled and gained strength. The new government closed all bank accounts, and everybody had to start on an equal basis. Forty Deutschmark (German marks) were allotted to each person. Companies were nationalized, factories stripped of machinery, typewriters and telephones carted off by the truckload. Railway lines were lifted so only one track was left, leaving no room for oncoming traffic. Large farms were divided into small parcels, sometimes going to factory workers who had no idea how to work the land. Whatever was harvested from this barren land had to be split with the Russians, who, of course, got the larger share and shipped some of it to Russia, which is notorious for its food shortages.

We were faced with a famine. My mother urged me to keep a diary to list the rations we received, and this is what we were given: 3 lb. of bread, 5 lb. of potatoes, and 150g of either rice, oats, or flour in a two-week period. A little jam, as well; but no vegetables, butter, or margarine were available.

Nothing was mentioned in my diary about fish, meat, or dairy products; but I remember getting either meat, fish, eggs, or cottage cheese on a weekly basis. And for this we had to stand in line for hours with our own containers to put it in. Milk was only for small children. Mother conscientiously assigned portions to us, particularly bread. We were given three or four slices per day, and it was up to each one of us to make it last through the day. Since we did not want to eat bread dry all the time, mother concocted a mixture of yeast flakes, onions and marjoram as a sandwich spread. To us it tasted like liverwurst, and we thought it was a delicacy. Black-market trade flourished.

The valuables people had not lost in bombing raids during the war were now lost by trading them in for food. Farmers became wealthy on all the silver, antiques, linens, and other valuables city dwellers exchanged for some food. A joke was that farmers had a clock on each wall and Persian rugs in the stables. Since our family had lost all our valuables, we had only liquors and wines to trade in. Fortunately, we established contact through a friend with a mill owner who loved good wines. My mother and I took turns driving to the village to exchange the wine for some flour, farina, vegetables, and sometimes some eggs. I dreaded those trips because the trains were overcrowded, as well as unreliable, and the walk from the mill to the train station seemed miles long with the heavy bags I had to carry.

Constantly I had to stop for rest, because I was out of breath, and my whole body ached from the heavy loads. Every time I made it home, it seemed like a miracle. Back then people had to push and shove to get into the train. Once I was pushed so hard from people in the back that I lost control and fell over a bumper, hanging loose with my arms and legs dangling in the air, holding onto my bags tightly and being weighted down by the knapsack on my shoulders. All I could do was scream for help, and to my great relief, some strong arms pulled me back by my feet until I found ground again. That was a frightful experience, but the extra food helped us to survive.

CHAPTER 13

My father was fortunate to have found a good position as the president of the only insurance company allowed in the district. His old company had been dissolved right after the war ended. Financially, we were well provided for.

Schools were open again, too. In 1945, the Russians had taken over our school building, and we were now located in the Bauhaus building. The Bauhaus had been built in 1925 by Walter Gropius, who is recognized worldwide as the founder of modern European architecture. He used cubic shapes in furniture, as well as in buildings. For external buildings, he used a lot of glass and steel as you find in many buildings today. Everything had to be functional. Hitler had closed the Bauhaus; and in 1937, Gropius fled to the United States where he became chairman of the Department of Architecture at Harvard University. My father was very fond of the Bauhaus style, and we had two rooms furnished by the Bauhaus. When my school friends came, I always felt embarrassed, because it was so different from what everybody else had.

While a number of our teachers had been dismissed because they were "politically unreliable," some had come back out of retirement and had trouble earning our respect. Actually, we were mean to them at times. One time we decided not to answer any questions in chemistry class. All of us complied until the teacher asked what the Bunsen burner was for; one girl giggled "to burn." Another time we decided to ignore a written test and leave the pages blank. I stuck to my promise but fell flat on my face when I later discovered that the others had filled out their papers after all. (To this day, I cannot abide people who say one thing and do another.)

No school books were available; even paper was scarce. Somehow, though, we managed to find enough paper to write everything down that our teachers taught us. This was our only resource material. We found ourselves writing our own school books. During the winter months, it was too cold to attend school in unheated classrooms, and we met only on Wednesdays and Saturdays to pick up homework. This became a habit until July, 1946. We received short instructions in school and had to do the actual work at home. Mostly we did this together with our friends. During this short time we were hardly able to understand our math homework because there was no time to explain it properly, and we really had to struggle. French and English proved to be a lot easier, or so I wrote in my diary. Sometimes we had to bring shovels and do cleanup work around the school. By the end of July, we had regular classes again, and I decided to add Latin to my language classes. In most subjects, I had to work hard to catch up with the others. Our school in Dessau was a lot more advanced then the boys' school in Ballenstedt had been. For the first time in my life, I became really ambitious and worked till I was again in the top group.

A lot of emphasis was put on history and politics. We students had no idea history could be presented in so many different ways. For example, Prussians under Hitler were heroes, while under the Communists, they were detested as militarists. Revolutions became heroic achievements under the Communists and were written about from their point of view. The different views we heard helped us to form our own opinions and not believe everything we were taught. We absorbed it all and kept quiet. We knew what happened to people who spoke up.

Several times we were taken to the movies to watch the horrors and crimes committed in KZ's (concentration camps). For four years we had lived through dangers, air raids, gunfire, and the screams of torture and rape; we just could not take any more. We believed what happened and had read and seen enough in the newspapers, but to watch it on the screen for an hour was more than we could bear. All the other horrors of the war still haunted us. So we hid our faces in our laps and covered our eyes and ears with our hands so we would not hear or see anything. Our teachers could force us to go to the movie, but they could not force us to watch, we thought.

In order to earn our ration cards, we all had to go into the ruins and clean bricks with a hammer every other Sunday. We became Truemmerfrauen (women in the rubble). It was dirty and hard work. After the bricks were cleaned, they had to be stacked up in the street so they would be picked up. Everywhere we looked, people were forming long chains and threw bricks to each other to speed up this process. Though we were wearing gloves, our hands became rough. To "rebuild Germany" was the idea, but lots of the bricks were shipped out of the country. All the manpower, though, hardly made a dent in the destruction around us. Whole street blocks had been demolished by bombs, and it was eerie.

However, we did our duty in order to receive our ration cards. Everything was rationed in those days, even gas and electricity. Both were turned on only a few times a day for a few hours, gas mainly around mealtimes, and sometimes not even long enough to finish cooking a meal. Little wood-burning stoves became popular items. Winters in Germany were bitterly cold, and even more so if families did not have enough coal to burn to keep at least one room warm. Though we had central heating, we never had enough coal to use it for years, and we made do with an emergency stove in the living room. Bedrooms had to stay cold. It felt good to snuggle into those big German featherbeds each night!

Another concern for mothers was the lack of fabrics. Linen had to be used over and over. When something tore it was mended or two pieces were sewn together. Clothes for growing children were a real problem. Old blankets were used for coats, parachute silk for dresses and blouses, and sheets were converted into dresses. When one of our Russian officers forgot to take his coat back with him to Russia, we dyed it; and I got a smaller coat out of it, which had to last for a long time. Clothes were passed from one person to another.

Since I did not have an older sister, I depended on my mother to give me some of her castoffs, which were a lot of her Paris fashions. After the German occupation of France, my father had taken her measurements to a Parisian couturier and ordered many beautiful dresses, suits, and coats for her. He liked women to be dressed elegantly, but my mother only wore it at his urgings and normally wore very subdued clothes. The result was that I inherited a lot of Mother's clothes. At my age, though, I felt overdressed and most uncomfortable in them. (How I would love to have them right now!) It was obvious those clothes were made for a woman, and I did not yet have the figure for it.

Shoes were also hard to come by. We outgrew them so fast that most of the time we wore some that did not fit us properly; mainly, they were too small. Wooden soles became popular, and we bought ribbons to nail on top of them, so we had summer shoes. Sometimes rubber shoes were on the market. They were very clumsy looking, and my feet perspired awfully. I never wore any of those, as Mother thought them too unhealthy.

With so many things lacking, the government was afraid of epidemics, and everybody had to undergo a series of inoculations periodically. In school we received vitamin pills, and later, one dry hard roll a day (we called them rocks).

However, it was not all work and hardship during these years. We had plenty of time to explore the countryside. My friend, Marianne, who lived only two houses away from us, and I took a lot of walks in the park which was only half a block away. On a spring day, we found ourselves deep in the park in front of a gate, which was open and led to a path going to the mausoleum which was located on a small island. It was a magnificent structure, like a small cathedral. Before the war, nobody had access to it because it belonged to the Dukes von Anhalt, and many of their ancestors were entombed there. We could not resist the temptation and crawled through a broken window. We found ourselves in a huge, dark hall with a high ceiling several stories high. In the rotunda, very high up, were stained-glass windows, which looked exceptionally beautiful. On the ground, elaborate caskets were lined up. On most of the caskets the covers had been lifted, and Marianne and I looked at the well-embalmed bodies of medieval princes and princesses in their gorgeous gowns and with headpieces that I had only seen in history books. The Russians must have thought they would find treasures in these caskets, and who knows, they might have found some jewelry, because we did not see any. In the past, this mausoleum must have been a beautiful resting place, but now it was in shambles. All of a sudden, while we were still inspecting it, we heard a sound from one of the balconies inside the building. Someone else must have been there and observed us. As fast as our feet would carry us, we climbed out of there and ran home.

CHAPTER 14

We now had reached an age when we needed to learn some social graces. Together with my friends, I started dancing lessons. Some of my friends even started to go "steady." None of the boys impressed me much, so I kept changing partners. Going home after dancing lessons was no romance either; we went in groups for safety, as sometimes couples were attacked and robbed in the dark.

We had a lot of house parties to practice dancing. Sometimes a group of girls came to our house, and we had more fun than we ever experienced before. Our spirits soared, and like all teenagers we enjoyed a good time together.

Soon the parties in our house had to cease. Word had gotten around that our mother-daughter tenants had moved, and we had room to spare. This time a Russian officer moved in. He was a captain and an engineer and obviously well-educated. He was quiet and treated us with respect. Once he asked my mother to prepare a meal so he could bring his friend over and both could learn German manners from my parents. All of the Russians were eager to learn "cultura" as they called it. He did not stay with us for long, and before we knew it, his room was occupied by a first lieutenant (Boris M.) who was in charge of the commissary. He was quite a different type. Not satisfied with one room, he took over the adjoining room, which was our dining room, as well.

And then the Russian parties started! And the girls kept coming! Deep into the night they drank and sang, laughed and danced. My mother also had to cook for Boris, and I did the shopping at the PX. I was apprehensive about this, but Boris had warned the soldiers to leave me alone, and nobody bothered me. He himself had to be careful how he treated our family, because, by then, all soldiers had strict orders to leave civilians alone. Fortunately, he was also protective of us. One night my friend, Helga, stayed late, and he had company. Our bathroom was located right across from his room, and we were concerned going to it alone. We decided that two were safer than one and went together. While we were inside we heard strange sounds in front of the door. Then came Boris' voice calling to somebody harshly. Now we knew we were safe and went back to the living room. When my mother cleaned up Boris' room the next morning, she found blood all over the place. When she asked him about it, his explanation was that a soldier was waiting to harm us, so he beat him up. Later this same soldier molested a Russian officer's wife, and because of this, he was executed.

Boris was rather amiable and never could be alone in his rooms for long. We got used to seeing him all over the house —in the kitchen with my mother and in the living room with father or with us. He was always fun and full of stories. Once his motorcycle (he called it "goat") was stolen, and we were worried about his reaction. Would he blame us? He never did, even when other items were stolen from his room. He just laughed it off and said, "So what, I'll just go and steal another one."

We resented the occupation troops, their molesting of women, and taking anything they took a fancy to without restraint. In no uncertain terms I told Boris we wished they would all go home and leave us alone. If we could not help our situation, at least I wanted to let the Russians know that we did not have any respect for them. My mother, who is a very gentle woman, was shocked and scared by my wild and free talk, thinking that surely one of these days they would come for me. To my surprise, I gained their respect. Our officer brought all kinds of people home telling them, "Sigrid can fix anything; she knows it all." Luckily, I was only faced with an officer who had a sunburned back; others needed some sewing, or someone to listen to their family problems.

Their flattery did not fool me though, and I was always on my guard. One night, my sister was visiting her foster parents, and I was sleeping alone. I woke up and saw a tall shadow in the open doorway. Every so often a cigarette lit up. I was stiff with fear. How would I get out of this situation? The best way was to treat it casually, as an everyday occurrence, I told myself. So I began making sounds as if I was just waking up and asked the shadow quietly who it was and what he wanted and to turn the lights on so I could see to whom I was talking. It was Boris. He had just come home from the movies and wanted to tell somebody about it. While I talked to him, I made my voice go louder so my parents, who slept next door, would wake up. And sure enough, my father appeared shortly after and told Boris he wanted to hear his story. I needed sleep because I had to go to school the next morning. So he went with my father and sat on my parents' bed for an hour talking. We could not avoid such situations. If we locked our doors, this was taken as a sign of our distrust, which made him angry. There was no telling what he would do if he lost his temper.

Usually none of us girls stayed alone in the apartment. One Sunday afternoon, however, I had a lot of homework and could not go for our regular walk in the park with my parents and sister. I was not worried because Boris was not at home, and we did not think he would appear anytime soon. This was poor judgment. After a while Boris did come home and, of course, searched the apartment to find somebody to talk to. When he entered the living room, I noticed he was quite drunk, and there was a strange gleam in his eyes that I had not seen before. I was immediately on my guard. After he talked a while, he grabbed me all of a sudden. I struggled free and threw anything in sight at him. With chairs overturned and rugs pushed aside, the room looked like a battlefield. I made it to the door and escaped across the street, hiding with a neighbor friend. There I stayed, watching behind the curtains for my parents to return. Only then did I go back home and could not have faced a friendlier scene than I found in the kitchen. Boris was talking and laughing with my parents and greeting me as the best of friends. Only the sly looks he shot in my direction told me he was scared of what I might say. Guilt was written all over his face, and he talked even more than usual. He knew I could have reported him to his superior, but I did not feel like creating a scandal. I would make sure he did not have a chance to find me alone again. I never told my parents about it, and they could not have suspected anything, as the living room was completely straightened out. He must have worked fast and hard to remove the evidence.

Events of a different nature took place which left us shaken and fearful for many of our friends and neighbors. One morning we woke up and found Russian trucks in front of almost every house in our street. Armed guards were in back and in front of the houses. What was the meaning of this again? Soon we found out. Boris' girlfriend came running, begging him to help her; she was supposed to go with her parents to Russia. Most of the engineers, technicians, and interpreters who had worked for the local Junkers aircraft plant were shipped to Russia. This included the families, visitors, and girlfriends that just happened to be in the houses of the engineers. Trucks were loaded with all their belongings to transport them. The girl's family belonged in that category. But Boris just shook his head and detached himself from this. How could he have had any influence anyway? Crying, she left, and we never saw her again.

My father's best friend had worked with V2 weapons, and we were worried about him. Soon they sent word that they also had to leave. There was no mercy. Nobody had suspected anything of this. We were all shaken up. What would happen next? Would we ever see our friends again?

For quite some time we were worried that the Russians might deport more people, and we lived with unease and fear. We were very suspicious of what the Russians might do next.

After living six years near Moscow, the deported families came back. Most of them had sold their belongings in Russia so they could buy some extra food. They had to start all over again.

My father's friend and his family returned also. They had suffered a lot of hardships, lack of food being one of them. A little girl, Rosi, had been born to them while they were near Moscow. Rosi suffered from malnutrition and was allowed to go to a Russian kindergarten, where she could be fed. Our family had just received a package from my aunt in Westphalia and among other things it had some chocolate. Intending to give Rosi a treat, mother gave her a piece of it. She looked at it, tasted it, and spit it out. The chocolate tasted so strange to her that she did not like it. She pointed at some cooked potatoes that were left over from our dinner and, after receiving one, was as happy as if she had received something very special.

CHAPTER 15

My girlfriend, Marianne, and her family had left our city and escaped over the border to West Germany. She wrote raving letters about conditions over there. My mother's family lived in Westphalia, West Germany, and their letters also told us of a new awakening to a better life. If only I could see some of this, I wished. In 1947, a neighbor woman planned to take a trip to the West, and I begged my parents to let me go with her. They gave their permission, and off Mrs. Reimer and I went. How we reached the West is somewhat hazy in my mind, as I just followed Mrs. Reimer and a group of others who wanted to cross the border. It seemed we walked an endlessly long time through the woods. Once we saw in the distance men with a stretcher, and somebody whispered, "There was trouble. A person probably has been shot. Keep quiet and hide." We did reach the West unharmed; each person traveled on to their destinations by train.

People on the Western side of the border were so cheerful, looked well-dressed and fed, and appeared so free of all burdens! After visiting relatives, I went to see Marianne near Frankfurt. This was American territory. We saw all the sights around Frankfurt, and it was great being with my friend again. We laughed and giggled all the time. When we even giggled in a movie theater, it rubbed a big black soldier the wrong way. We had not noticed him, but suddenly he stood in front of us and shouted in German, "Why are you laughing so silly? I have more money than you!" We understood his German, only what money had to do with laughing was beyond our understanding. In no time at all two MP's appeared and grabbed him. What a relief! That stopped our silly laughing. Soon my trip into a different world ended, and I found myself back home and in school again. Boris was still with us.

One day our school secretary called me out of class and told me to go home immediately. My mother had problems with Boris. When I reached home, there was a turmoil. Boris had been ordered back to Russia and was packing not only his belongings but ours as well. My poor mother watched helplessly. When I got home he had to deal with me. I called him all the bad names I could think of, and we wound up in a shouting match. I felt like a tigress defending her young. We had lost already so much and now this—no way! How much he finally got away with, we never really found out, but it could not have been much, as I got hold of most of it.

As soon as the rooms were vacant, we were already confronted with another boarder. Lt. Wassily R. was from Siberia and just a boy compared to the others. He gave us back one room, so we had more space, and he did not make any demands on my mother. The drinking parties and flow of visitors stopped. Only one friend, whom we called the "little captain" because he was so short, appeared all the time. He owned a Studebaker, which was his pride and joy. I had never seen an American car before. They told me where it was parked, and to make sure to go and take a look at it. American cars were showpieces, much admired and the owners envied. Actually I was disappointed; it was not as huge and flashy as I had expected.

In later years I was told that during the International Fair in Leipzig a super-modern American car was parked in the marketplace. Half of the population was gathered around admiring so much beauty. One man simply could not stay quiet and said, "What a beautiful Russian car this is. I have never seen such a gorgeous Russian car before." Somebody kicked him and said, "Man, don't you know an American car?" "Sure I do, but do I know you?" replied the other.

Like all the other Russian officers, Wassily wanted to feel a part of the family. If you met Russians on a personal basis and did not get into political discussions, they were a warm and fun-loving people, ambitious to learn as much as possible. This officer took correspondence courses in law and was always studying when he was at home, which was not very often. Since his room was vacant so much, he offered it to me for my studies. I was going into final exams and could not find a peaceful corner to study, so I took him up on it. Sometimes he came home early and just sat in another corner doing his own work. Often we wound up in serious conversations, and eventually we became friends. Once he managed to buy some coals for us, but they had to be delivered to a Russian-occupied house in the closed-off district. My friend, Helga, her brother and I managed to smuggle them out at night with a hand drawn-wooden wagon. We felt like thieves in the night and were scared stiff, but at least we helped our families.

Wassily did not stay long with us. By that time, all Russians were supposed to live in the closed-off district. Too much contact with Germans evidently was not considered good for their morale. Politically, we still were not trusted.

CHAPTER 16

In June, 1948, final exams for the "Abitur" (Matriculation) started. This was not too difficult, and we were prepared. Oral exams were the most feared. We had no idea which subjects we would be examined in and needed to be prepared for all.

Representatives from the Communist government were present, and we knew a lot of politics would come up. We also were aware we had to tell them what they wanted to hear in order to pass the exam. We were resigned to do the necessary. At least school would be over, and we could pursue our own interests. One of my classmates, however, stated she was not going to pretend and that she was going to tell her true opinions. She did and failed the exam. A day later she jumped from the roof of the school and was dead.

When it was my turn to be examined, I was questioned in geography and history. My topic in history was "Why did the Revolution in 1848 fail, and what were the successes in spite of it?" In geography I had to explain the transportation system in Europe. I passed. On July 17, we all received our diplomas.

As soon afterwards as possible, my friend, Helga, and I took a well-deserved (so we felt) vacation in Binz at the Baltic Sea. In my diary, I noted how food was our biggest problem. We were hungry all the time, because some days we were not able to get any bread. Our school days over, we had to face the real world and get prepared to find a job. Universities were overcrowded, and laborers' and farmers' children got preference in being accepted. With our degree (which equaled two years' college in the USA), we could get jobs as teachers, who were badly needed. However, most of us did not want to be under political pressure. If teaching did not suit us, the government decided we should become locksmiths. As "capitalistic" daughters, this was supposed to break our spirits and put us on the same level with laborers.

My greatest desire was to become a nurse. During one summer vacation, I had taken care of a partially paralyzed elderly lady. Her joy and gratitude touched me so much that I really felt I had something to give to people; and, by caring for others, I felt worthwhile and fulfilled. My father resented the idea completely. No daughter of his was waiting on others; they were to be waited on. If I was interested in the medical field, I could study medicine. I was not scientifically inclined, though, and I felt physicians did not have the personal relationship with their patients that nurses did. This is what attracted me to it.

Finally, my father decided I should become a photographer, because it was his hobby, and he thought I might have inherited some of his talent. I was enrolled in a technical college in West Berlin but had to wait six months for an opening. I had a choice to either working for my father or working for a seamstress. My friend, Helga, chose to take a job with my father's company, but I had no desire to be the boss's daughter. I took a job with the seamstress instead. No female in our family knew anything about sewing. We always had a seamstress do it for us. But times were changing, and I felt it would come in handy later on in life if I could make at least some of my clothes. This was not the most exciting time of my life but, without a doubt, very useful.

CHAPTER 17

In 1948, the currency reform in West Germany took place and accomplished miracles. Overnight, stores were filled with anything you needed or desired. Communists frowned on the West. After all, Germans did not accomplish this change; it was the Marshall Plan that made it all possible. The Marshall Plan (named after General George C. Marshall, American Secretary of State) was put into action in 1947 to accelerate European recovery from the ruins of the war. It gave massive American economic aid to Germany, as well as other European countries. Russia resented this plan. As we were told over and over again, East Germany was too proud to accept any foreign aid. They would accomplish the rebuilding of the country on their own with German workers and German financial resources.

The story of this western miracle reached us in the East. When our aunts in Westphalia invited my sister and me for a visit in 1949, we jumped at the opportunity. This was going to be a completely different trip than the one I took with the neighbor in 1947. A truck driver, who made frequent trips to Halle (East

Germany), was supposed to bring passes for us and drive us back. It was only a short trip by train to Halle from our home. We stayed with my mother's childhood friend in Halle and waited for the truck driver. When after two days no one came to claim us, we gave up the idea of waiting for a ride. I told my sister that I was going anyway; and if she wanted to come along, she could join me. Of course, she wanted to go with me! We studied the map and decided on a certain village near the border from where we would try our luck.

In Magdeburg, we had to change trains and were sitting in the waiting room counting our money (our parents thought we did not need much, as our trip had been paid for), when a young man joined us at the table. Watching our efforts, he asked if we were in financial trouble. He looked trustworthy, and we confided in him. The young man happened to be going in the same direction, only not across the border, but he said that he would see if he could spot a group that would take us along. He was true to his word, and even covered up for us when the police questioned everybody on the train as to their destination. We were with him, he said. At the last stop, he talked to a few women who looked prepared for a long walk. We could go with them, he told us. We were grateful to him and felt sorry to see him go in another direction.

It was a dark and rainy night. Mostly we followed the street; but when car lights came our way, we hid in the ditches of potato fields. It was so wet and muddy, we looked like tramps after awhile. When we came closer to the border, we had to leave the street and walk through the woods. Occasionally we heard patrol dogs barking and saw watchtowers. The women obviously knew their way, and we avoided all obstacles. Finally, we reached a clearing in the woods, a wide strip of grass, which was no-man's-land. It was visible from watchtowers and was the most dangerous part of our journey. "Run for your life," somebody called out, and we literally did.

Reaching the other side, everybody began to relax and talk. Hardly a word had been exchanged within this group before for fear somebody could hear us. We had been so tense that no one had wanted to talk anyway.

The worst was definitely over, but we still had a long way to go to reach Westphalia. We barely had any money, and we had to hitchhike. For a while we were in luck. Big trucks loaded people like cattle and gave them rides. Most people had sandwiches to eat because they were prepared for such a trip, but we had nothing. When they saw this and offered us some food, we were embarrassed and said we were not hungry. Shortly before Hanover, we were stuck and could not find a ride. We had to take the train. For an emergency like this I had saved the little money we had, and now it came in handy. My sister fussed; she was thirsty. I would not let her drink out of water faucets because they looked too dirty. Instead, I bought her a lemon to suck on, thinking that this would last longer than a soft drink.

Arriving in Hanover, we were overwhelmed by the cleanliness, the bustling traffic, and the elegance of the city. We looked at our mud-spattered and shabby clothes. I wore a new coat, but the material was so poor that in the rain it had shrunk to half its size. We felt like hiding in some hole. In order to get through the city we had to take a streetcar and then walk to the next highway. We did not dare sit on the seats in the car but stood outside on the platform. We felt and looked like outcasts. From then on, we did not have any trouble getting rides. The last pickup truck that stopped for us was loaded with people coming from a business outing. They were in jolly spirits and stopped at a restaurant. Without questioning us, they ordered two big Westphalian ham platters for us. All of a sudden we realized how hungry we were. We had not eaten for two days, and this was already the night of the second day on the road. Gisela sat in front of her platter and started to cry, "How can I eat this? My mother at home doesn't have anything like it." I figured mother would be glad for us to have the opportunity for such a feast.

The men in the truck drove us a few miles out of their way to deliver us straight to my aunt's doorstep. For two weeks we could eat and drink to our hearts' content. It was unbelievable! My sister's godmother bought her a pair of shoes. For the first time in my life, I saw a shoe store filled with boxes of shoes. Customers had a choice!

Everybody treated us so well. My cousins could not hear enough of all that had happened to us. One of them told me, "You ought to write a book; we never experienced anything like this." At that point it was the furthest thing from my mind.

Our vacation passed only too quickly, and we had to be on our way home.

Surely it would be easy enough to join a group going back, we figured. However, when we reached the border, there was no group, only a single woman with a little boy clutching his teddy bear. We talked to the West German border patrolman, and he said hardly anybody was going in our direction. We were more or less on our own. I liked challenges and was not afraid. I even asked the mother to join us, after I noticed that she lacked the courage to go on her own. Somehow I would find a way! The easiest path to follow would have been to walk along the side the street, since we did not know the territory at all. I made my sister and the woman wait behind some trees while I set out to explore on my own. Soon I ran into some policemen whose dogs barked viciously. They had stopped a car and did not notice me. So I crawled back to the others and told them that this way would be out of the question. We would have to stick to the woods. We walked for hours in an eastward direction without hearing or seeing a soul. We followed our instincts and hoped for a road sign. We finally detected one and, by moonlight, saw the name of a village. We followed the sign and miraculously found a deserted train station. It was so lonely and eerie that we hid under potato sacks that were on the floor. Once in a while we heard heavy footsteps belonging either to a policeman or a soldier, but we did not dare to peek. A train finally arrived; we got on and had a smooth ride home.

When we were back in Dessau, we were bursting to tell about our adventures but had to keep quiet. We would be in trouble if anyone found out we had gone to the West.

CHAPTER 18

I dreaded leaving my home and my school friends. But in September, 1949, I finally made the break and found myself alone at a technical college in West Berlin to begin my training as a photographer. It did not take long to make new friends, mainly with other girls from the East who, like myself, lived within walking distance from the school.

During the first weeks of our arrival, we all were invited to a newcomers' coffee with the directress. As it happened, after coming home from school, my landlady called me to her living room. She had company and offered me a glass of wine. I had never had any wine before, so I treated it like water. After two glasses, I found myself in high spirits and happy as a lark. I had to go to the coffee in this condition. Everybody was serious, subdued, and uncomfortable with each other—until I arrived on the scene. My happy and carefree attitude broke the ice, and in no time, we all relaxed. During the coffee, the other students made me sit next to the directress, as nobody else wanted this honor! In my condition, I would have done anything I was asked to do! Since I had lost my shyness for the day, I really entertained her, so much so, that she later asked a friend if I always talked so much. I wish I could remember all I said!

All students from East Germany were in the same financial shape—poor! East Deutschmarks (DM)70 were exchanged into West DM for students on a one to one basis once a month; all other funds had to be exchanged at the rate of 1:4 or 1:5, depending on the exchange rate of the day. Rent and food were expensive. So were photographic papers, films, and chemicals. Through the American Care program, all students were provided with a warm lunch each day, consisting mainly of soup brought in huge buckets. This truly helped, and we were grateful for the meals. The American Care program was also a big help to needy people by sending them packages of food. The disadvantage was that you had to have relatives in the United States who ordered it and paid for it. My friend, Helga, had relatives in New York who sent frequent packages to them, and she told me about it.

Many times my friends and I took the subway to the Eastern sector of Berlin, where we bought any food we could find. Going back and forth, we were subject to inspection by the police. Luckily, we always passed.

As prospective photographers, we were frequently on assignments and got to know and love Berlin, especially its people, parks, and architecture. We raced to every news event, boldly pushing through the crowd with reporters, and the police just grinned when we showed our student passes.

For one of our architectural photographs, my roommate and I drove to Potsdam and got permission to take pictures inside the imperial palace in the gardens of Sans Souci. Regular tours passed quite often, interrupting us, but we were so absorbed in our work, we did not notice when the flow of visitors stopped. Then, when we were trying to leave the ballroom, we found the doors locked. Although there was access to other rooms, we could not get out. Spending the night here will be a great adventure, we thought. We tried out several couches but found them too short to stretch out on and too hard to put our heads down. We preferred to find a way out, rather than go through with our original plan. From the balcony, we could not see a soul, as it was getting dark by then, and most people had gone home. Our shouts finally attracted the attention of a man who got help, and in no time we were on our way home.

CHAPTER 19

I went home every other weekend and sometimes returned to Berlin with a neighbor girl, Ruth. Ruth was engaged to a young man from the suburb in East Berlin in which the Russian headquarters was located. While waiting on the platform for the subway to arrive one day, the "little captain," Wassily's friend, appeared all of a sudden. He was just as startled to see me as I was startled to see him. "Stay right here, I'll be right back," he urged me; and in no time, he came back with Lt. Wassily, who was also stationed there. I never dreamed I would meet those two again. Since Russian soldiers were not allowed to have any connections with Germans, we could not be seen speaking together. We went to a bandstand in a park close by, which protected us from the snow. Since Berlin was still a little strange to me, it was good to have somebody to talk to about home and the old days. Wassily had been in several other cities in East Germany before coming to Berlin and evidently had been on the move quite a bit. Wassily and I met a few times after that, mostly walking in a small park close to the subway station because it was too cold to sit down anywhere. As brief as these meetings were, they did not pass unnoticed, so it seems. One evening, after we said goodbye at the entrance to the park, I watched him crossing the street. A uniformed figure appeared out of the shadows, followed him, and walked away with him. I never saw him again.

A few months later, Ruth and I were arrested. Our train from Dessau had been late getting to Berlin, and we were in a hurry to get to her fiance's birthday party. We did not have time to leave our luggage at my place and had to take our suitcases with us to Karlshorst. No taxis were available in those days, so we had to walk from the subway station to her in-laws. On the way to their house, we missed a turn and found ourselves on a strange street. We knew we were lost and walked back. Before we got out of that street, however, a KGB agent in civilian clothes appeared out of nowhere. He put his hand heavily on my shoulder and said, "Frau, why are you walking here? Come with me." Paralyzed with fear, we followed him. On the way to the police station we met a German policeman, whom he asked to come along. Later it was explained to us that he could not have arrested us on his own but had to have a German official with him. We did not know this, though it would not have made any difference to us since we were so frightened of him. Pointing to us, he told the policeman, "These are spies from the West." Arriving at the police station, he again accused us of being spies from West Berlin. We gave the address we had been looking for and explained the circumstances, but they did not believe us. Ruth's uncle was president of the electric company in East Berlin and politically trusted. We gave them his name, and they called him, only to be told he was in an important meeting that night and could not be disturbed. We were really out of luck. Our passports were checked and seemed in order, but they still had doubts.

Every time a person moved, he or she had to report the new address to the police, who kept a record of everybody's whereabouts. Luckily, my passport still showed my address in Dessau. When I moved to West Berlin, I had forgotten to have it changed. (However, my mother had reported my move to Berlin in my absence.) Next, they tried to call the police in Dessau to see if any change of address had been reported. My friend would be all right, I knew, but this was the end for me. Nobody could help me now, I thought. But the Lord must have been on my side. The telephone lines were always busy, and the policemen did not get through. I thought of my camera in my suitcase and prayed they would not search it. This definitely would incriminate me as a spy. After all attempts failed to contact family or get more evidence, the policeman finally asked the KGB officer what they were supposed to do with us. In disgust he threw down his cigarette and said, full of contempt, "Let'em go. We will catch up with them sooner or later after we contact the police in Dessau, and they show a change of address to Berlin." After he left, we asked the policeman what could have happened to us. He opened the window and showed us the prison on the other side. "This place is full of cases like yours, all kept on spy charges with little proof. Most of them will go to Siberia. You are the lucky ones." We were afraid to leave the building in case the KGB man would be waiting for us outside. Ruth and I asked for somebody to take us to the train station, which they did. We had no more desire to attend any birthday party. We were just glad to be free. From then on, every trip I took home was a nightmare, because they could have picked me up at any time. I never told my parents or my sister, so they would not worry about me. I just found excuses not to go home so often.

CHAPTER 20

Having gone to an all-girls' school most of my life, I was very shy with boys or young men. When modeling for a classmate in our studio, the instructor shouted at me, "Is this the way you look at young men?" To my embarrassment, the door was half open, and the brother of my classmate had overheard everything. Obviously amused, he asked me for a date. Heinz was a medical student from Dresden studying in Rostock, East Germany, and only came for short visits to see his brother in Berlin. He was handsome, intelligent, and had a good sense of humor. Though we dated quite a while, I soon became aware that he liked all girls in general. Heinz and his brother financed their studies by buying photographic lenses in East Germany and selling them at a good profit in West Berlin. This trade was illegal. On one of these trips back from Dresden, Heinz was caught and imprisoned. He served several months and was finally released under the condition that he finish his medical studies and never leave East Germany. He was fortunate that they needed physicians so badly! Soon after he was released, he was back in West Berlin and came to visit me. He was pale, but his spirits were not broken. After he graduated, he did manage to escape to the West and now practices gynecology in a southern German town.

Heinz had introduced me to a friend of his from Rostock, Dan, who had transferred to the Free University in Berlin, because Berlin was his hometown. A lot of my memories are connected with Dan. We took motorcycle rides all over town and went to balls and more parties. A number of foreign students visited him, and he brought them over so I could meet them. They were quite interesting to talk to, and we had a good time. Dan also took me to many students' affairs. A favorite meeting place was around the swimming pool in the Olympic Stadium. A whole group of medical students got together there, not only for relaxation, but mostly for serious discussions and an opportunity to share each other's problems. Many were from the East and struggling on their own. They were cut off from their families and worried about them.

Dan was one of the most trustworthy persons I have ever met. Many of my friends consulted him with medical problems. My friends told me about their problems, but I would never mention to Dan that I knew about it, and he never

"Is this the way you look at young men?" The instructor reprimanded me.

Ruins of the Viktoria Luise Platz in Berlin

discussed it. Dan performed research for one of his studies, and we rejoiced with every mouse that survived and bemoaned every one that died. We had a unique friendship; though, unfortunately, I could only love him as a friend.

Love came to me in the way of my landlady's grandson, Peter. One day in 1951, when I opened the door, he stood there. He had come to see his grandmother, and she was not at home. Not knowing him, I did not let him in and sent him on his way. But somehow he made an impression on me even then. When we were finally introduced by his grandmother, we liked each other and started dating. Peter was in his final exams from medical school, and I had only a few months left to graduate. When he invited me to spend my vacation with him at his parents' house, I was at first hesitant; after all, I barely knew him. However, his grandmother persuaded me to accept the invitation.

It was a decision I never regretted. His parents were lovely and made me feel at home. Their house was located close to a lake, and we went swimming, fishing, and sailing all the time. I had come from an area which did not have any lakes worth mentioning. The Elbe River in Dessau was the closest we had come to water. The Brandenburg lake country was all new to me, and it was beautiful. Peter knew all the lakes we sailed, and I just drifted along enjoying the feeling of being so close to him. He taught me a few tricks about sailing, which came in handy one day when I was caught alone in the boat. Peter had left me, briefly, and had tied the boat to a pole. Suddenly, the boat broke loose, and I was on my own in an area that was surrounded by wooden planks. Fortunately, Peter saw what was happening and shouted instructions at me. I made a beautiful turn and landed exactly where he was standing on a plank. For a novice like me, this was truly a miracle; and of course, I was relieved that nothing had happened to the boat.

Another time we were sailing and stopped at a dock where the yacht of East German government officials was anchored. Peter was interested in looking at it; and when he heard that one of the ministers had serious burn wounds, he offered to treat him. While he was gone, I had to stay in the boat under observation. The guards later offered us a ride in their boat, which we accepted. It was not as luxurious as I had expected it to be, but very nice.

During the ride, we met a number of sightseeing boats, and the curious and dour looks the people sent our way made me feel very uncomfortable. We also had to hide the fact that I resided in West Germany. Automatically, we were careful around Communists.

We spent several summers with his parents in this way. We wrote and dated for three years. Unfortunately, circumstances would cause us to drift apart. My family would flee to Hamburg from East Germany, while he would remain in East Berlin with a heavy work load as a resident physician. He was studying a new surgical procedure under a famous professor and could not give it up to move to the West. Several years later he married a girl from his hometown. I am glad he found happiness in life and satisfaction in his successful medical career.

In the summer of 1994, I saw Peter again. Though we had not seen each other in decades, I felt a special bond still existed between us—a comfortable familiarity. Together with his mother, we laughed over and exchanged many common experiences. We had two wonderful days to reminisce and parted as good friends.

During our reunion, I questioned Peter about Heinz, the medical student I had met in Berlin. I knew Heinz practiced gynecology in the same city as Peter. He laughed; it was so ironic. Peter had hired Heinz, and they had worked together for many years. How small the world is!

CHAPTER 21

The year 1950 brought a lot of changes to my family in Dessau. My father was under a lot of pressure from the Communists to show support for them and to make speeches on their behalf. He refused to do that and soon was declared politically untrustworthy. Finally, he was ousted and had to look for another job. At least, this was the story my sister and I were told. However, during a visit to Germany in 1994, I was given a letter that my father had written to his brother on December 7, 1950. In it he explained the true reason for his ouster, and how he was set up by the Communists to commit a "crime." One of his employees had made remarks against the Communist government in my father's presence. My father pretended not to have heard so the employee would not get into trouble, and he did not report it. This was the wrong thing to do. In his position, it was required of him to report anybody making anti-communistic remarks. But he was an honorable man and never could have been an informer. He had fallen into a trap, and it cost him his job. He also told his brother that he survived the GESTAPO persecution, so he would have no trouble surviving the STASI persecution, as well. Survival in East Germany, however, was not to be. This event would be the major turning point in my family's life.

Every time my father found a good position, it was refused to him because he was on the blacklist. We did not have a choice but to leave, and we secretly prepared to relocate in the West. My trips home became more frequent again, and I returned to Berlin with suitcases loaded with linens, household goods, and books. All suitcases were searched before getting to Berlin. I constantly worried about passing inspection and being able to carry the heavy loads. The suitcases were so heavy that I could only carry them from one street block to another. It was sheer torture, and lots of times I thought I could not go another step. My father was obsessed with saving his books at any cost. My mother, though, had pity and lots of times sneaked some books back out to lessen the burden. How I dreaded these trips and the physical pain connected with it! From Berlin, these items were mailed to our relatives in Westphalia.

Finally, my father arrived in Berlin to try to find a way to reach the West by plane. Some people sold their passports at a high price, and once the buyers reached the West safely, they mailed them back to the rightful owners. Passports had pictures, so he had to find somebody that at least resembled him slightly. We found such a person. However, when Father was going through passport control at the airport, each person was asked to sign their name, and the signature was compared with the one on the passport. He was not prepared for this. The authorities must have caught on to the "passport trick" and started catching people with signatures. I felt desperate when I saw the police leading my father away. What would happen to him? Fortunately, he returned late in the afternoon and stayed in a spare bedroom of my landlady's for several weeks until he received a visa. He had connections with several large insurance companies in the West, and one of them hired him as personnel director and arranged for his visa. He was never really happy in this job because he was not in charge of everything. It was in his nature to be the boss.

My mother and sister had stayed in Dessau so my sister could finish school.

It was only a matter of weeks before she graduated. During her last visit to our grandmother in Leipzig to say good-bye, the police came to our house in Dessau looking for my mother. She was visiting with the seamstress at the time. When mother returned home, neighbors told her about the visit, and they all decided it would be best for her to go into hiding. If it was a serious matter, they would be back. Hurriedly she packed a few items in a suitcase and went to stay with our cook. Later that day, our cook questioned our neighbors about what had happened. The police had indeed come back and had questioned everybody in the neighborhood about what they knew of our family. They wanted to know where my father was and where I was. They suspected we had defected to the West. My mother never went back to our house. She took a train that night to a city where we had friends. She dared not go directly to Berlin, as those cars were always searched thoroughly, and they would look for her there. Hoping to spend the night with friends in Zerbst, she went to their house, but nobody heard her ringing the doorbell nor opened the door. She spent all night on their doorsteps.

Late the next morning, she arrived in Berlin. Our school secretary called me to the office, where I found my mother close to a nervous breakdown. She was shaking and could barely talk. I did not need to ask any questions; her ordeal was written all over her face.

Now we were worried about Gisela in Leipzig. No telephone connection existed between West Berlin and East Germany, and I had to find a trustworthy friend in East Berlin from where I could call my uncle. But would he cooperate and send my sister to Berlin immediately? He was a devout Communist and occupied such a high position that he received birthday cards from party leaders in Berlin. He understood the situation perfectly. Maybe he did not even want to harbor a "wanted person." He personally drove Gisela with his chauffeur to the railroad station. I wonder if the chauffeur would have cooperated if he knew he was aiding a refugee! What a relief that we all had escaped! My father sent us the necessary papers, and my mother and sister departed for our new home in Hamburg (where they still are today). I stayed behind to finish and pass exams.

With Princess Annette at The Industrial Fair in Hanover

And on vacation in the Netherlands

PRINCESS HUNTS FOR A HUSBAND

A PRINCESS who made up her mind to marry a rich Texas rancher moved into the ritziest hotel in Dallas. Then she sat back to wait for suitors.

Princess Alexandra von Anhalt, 52, told local newspapers and television stations about her search this month — and the ranchers came flocking in.

Out of 50 early callers, the princess — a fan of the Dallas TV show — almost chose two.

"But I found out one was already married," she says. "And I almost married the other one, but at the last minute I decided my heart wasn't in it."

The German princess first planned to wed a rancher when she came to Texas on a visit in 1965

"I decided then I must go home and leave my husband (a German veterinarian) and find a Texas rancher," she

VON ANHALT and nephew: "I must find a rancher."

says. "I need a man who will offer me his arm when we walk and I need him to have lots of land and even a horse for me."

She says her family thinks she is crazy, but "German husbands are not so nice to their wives. And Texas ranchers will let me go out on the ranch and ride the horses."

Her nephew, Prince Jurgen von Anhalt, who accompanied the princess on her American quest, says: "Wedding bells are ringing. She will have a husband soon.

"There are so many coming through the door that it's leaving her breathless.

"So far, a Houston rancher has flown her to a rodeo, another has taken her to his ranch, a man from El Paso flew in to marry her immediately, and several others have taken her to dinner."

She feels she is ideally suited to be a rancher's wife. She says she has a master's degree in agriculture and has won hundreds of horseback riding prizes.

But the biggest problem her rancher husband may have is how to introduce his new wife.

Her full name is Princess Marie-Antoinette Elizabeth-Alexandra Irmgard Edda Charlotte Anhalt.

She never found the "right" husband

CHAPTER 22

It was with deep regret that I left Berlin and all my friends to join my parents and sister in Hamburg in 1951. My experience with Berliners was so different from the people in Hamburg. Berliners were friendly and had a wonderful sense of humor. In Hamburg, however, people were cold natured and suspicious of refugees.

As newcomers, it was difficult to find a place to live. Fortunately, my father had connections, and we found a one-bedroom apartment which was a far cry from what we had been used to. My sister and I had to sleep in the living room on a couch and cot which had to be made up every night. We always looked forward to weekends when Gisela and I could sleep in the bedroom. Beds felt so good after sleeping like that for some time! Fortunately this state of affairs did not last long, and we soon found a two-bedroom apartment which was more comfortable in every way.

Hamburg is a beautiful city with many lakes and nice parks. It also was located in an area where we had many visitors driving through on their way to the North Sea. In general, it brought us more in touch with the western world.

I also had the good fortune to hear about my friend from Ballenstedt, the Princess Marie Antoinette von Anhalt. I visited her when she lived in a Lutheran home for children. She had come there as a patient originally and stayed on as a help to the sisters. She told me what had happened to her family after we left. Her father was arrested for being an aristocrat, landowner and capitalist and was put in a concentration camp that the Communists were now using for their prisoners. Somebody who had been imprisoned with him later told newspapers that the Duke had to clean stairs with a toothbrush and had starved to death.

Hearing of her father's death, Annette had a mental breakdown and was not aware of her surroundings for some time. She had recovered by the time I met her. Her mother, brothers, sisters, and a faithful servant had all escaped to the West. When crossing the border, they were caught, and all valuables were taken away from them. For a while, they lived on donations from friends; later, they had access to investments the Duke's financial advisers had made in the West.

Annette and I stayed in touch for a few years and spent some vacations together. During my first year in the United States, we corresponded regularly but then lost touch with each other. Friends and family kept sending me newspaper clippings about the Princess's activities. She was constantly having financial difficulties and made headlines with the jobs she took to earn money. She sang in supermarkets, owned a bar, sold pictures in the streets of Berlin, and hired herself out as a high-paid maid. In a desperate effort to come by cash, she "adopted" thirty commoners who wanted to be elevated to nobility. The Duke's only surviving son said that there are more adopted "von Anhalts" than the true blue bloods. (Prince Eduard tried to introduce a bill with the Bundestag in Bonn to put a stop to this practice, but I never read that he succeeded.)

In one last effort to establish herself through a prosperous marriage, Annette flew to Texas and advertised that she was on the lookout for a "Texan." I was surprised to find a clipping about this in an American newspaper. A friend told me she had heard Annette being interviewed on television's Real People. I wish I could have seen it! Though she was considered the black sheep of the family, I personally remember her as a dear friend and a warmhearted, compassionate, generous human being. She was also a lot of fun.

In 1992, the Princess Marie Antoinette, Edda Charlotte, Elizabeth, Alexandra von Anhalt died a lonely woman of cirrhosis of the liver.

CHAPTER 23

As soon as I arrived in Hamburg, I started looking for a job. No one was waiting for a photographer from Berlin! As my first job, I worked in a color laboratory. My colleagues were very nice but did not dare to speak up about poor conditions for fear they might lose their jobs. One after another fainted and got sick due to the lack of fresh air; there was no ventilator and no air conditioning. During lunch break, the windows were opened to improve this condition; however, when there are six people working in one small room, the air gets stale fast. After I saw another woman collapse, I was determined to remedy this situation. I stormed to the boss and gave him a piece of my mind. He was sitting at his desk looking at pornographic pictures, and it made me sick. What I said did not disturb him, and he calmly fired me. That night I told my father what I had done, and he approved wholeheartedly. Father even went so far as to call the Health Department and reported these bad conditions. They inspected the laboratory, and changes occurred very soon after. I became a hero to the remaining employees, and I was glad that I could help them work in a healthier environment.

It did not take long to find another job—this time as an industrial photographer. With the help of another employee who had taken pictures before I came, I had a free hand in furnishing a darkroom and studio. This was what I called fun! I loved my job, but once in a while my "poor refugee" status came up, and it was demeaning to me. When I had a chance to go to the United States, I felt I should give it a try.

Die Bundesrepublik Deutschland und die
Deutsche Demokratische Republik 1949 – 1989

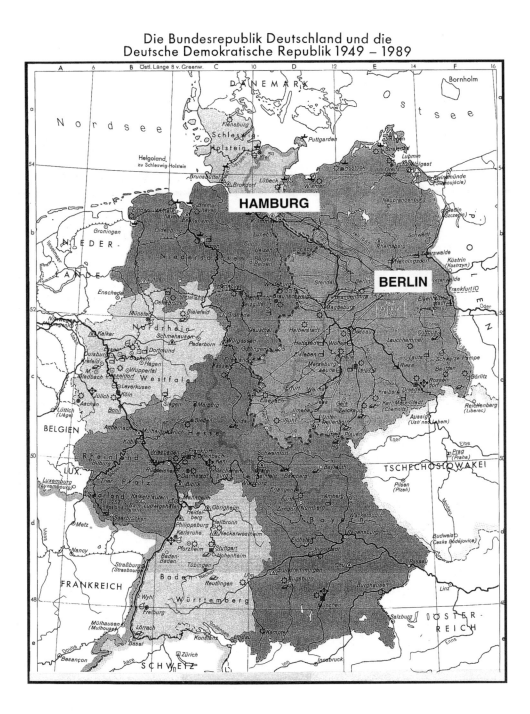

NEW HORIZONS

PART II

I confess that the first years in my life were more dramatic than the ones I am about to share. However, my past is irrevocably intertwined with the present and, therefore, both parts are necessary to understand my life.

While my life under Hitler and Communism was one of passivity, where we all blindly followed our leaders, I am now free to pursue my own interests and follow my conscience.

CHAPTER 24

AMERICA THE BEAUTIFUL, LAND OF OPPORTUNITIES—here I come...

On a clear, sunny day in December, 1956, I arrived at Idlewild Airport in New York. I was greeted by a lot of noise and confusion.

I was picked up by Dr. Smith and driven to my hotel in downtown Manhattan. (Dr. Smith was the representative of the company in Germany where I had taken advertising pictures, and he had helped me come to the U.S.A.) My first reaction to Manhattan was shock. My hotel room was dark because of all the skyscrapers surrounding the hotel, and the hotel was not too clean. Nothing was what I had expected. What had brought me here?

In Hamburg, I had been a photographer with a telephone company. As such, I had done a lot of advertising and technical photos for customers around the world. In this capacity I met representatives from various countries and discussed with them their need for pictures. Most of them were friendly and interesting. Among those was Dr. Smith, the U.S. representative. While Dr. Smith was in Hamburg, my assistant and her daughter decided to emigrate to Canada and urged me to go with them. I always was adventurous, but starting a new life in another country would not be easy. I investigated the opportunities available in the New World.

Actually, I was happy with my job. I had a studio, darkroom; and when outside pictures were required, a chauffeur to drive me to the various locations. And then Trautchen, my assistant, was always there when it got hectic. It was a glamourous job but did not pay very much. It was time to move on. I still lived with my parents and wanted to be on my own and be responsible for myself. So I needed to make a change and going to a different country might just be the answer. I questioned Dr. Smith about the prospects in Canada, since he was a Canadian citizen living in New York. He suggested that, if I wanted to go to anywhere, to go to the United States.

There was another reason why it was so important to come to the U.S. Dr.

Smith had fallen in love with me and wanted me to be with him in New York. Dr. Smith was Hungarian and Jewish. He had spent time in the Bergen Belsen concentration camp, and his health was not very good. He sent frantic letters to me to hurry up and come. He felt that his health might deteriorate more, and he wanted me to be part of his life as long as possible. I did not take this too seriously and thought he just could not wait for me to come. However, I did depart for the U.S. as soon as I had my visa. Looking back on it now, I think he must have had a premonition of what would happen to him.

To obtain a permanent visa, my first step was to go to the U.S. Consulate. I discovered that the main requirement was a sponsor who would be responsible for me. A sponsorship is a matter of trust, as the immigrant can get into trouble with the law and become heavily in debt. The sponsor would have to bail his protege out. Of course, Dr. Smith tried everything to find me a sponsor, and a few weeks later, I received an affidavit from a friend of his—a wealthy and prominent physician in New York. The ball started rolling; and in December, 1956, shortly before Christmas, I was on my way via Lufthansa to New York.

Strange sounds greeted me on my arrival in New York City, and I could not understand much. Everybody was in a hurry. People shoved and pushed their way into subways. Ladies in mink coats sat in the subway noisily chewing gum with their mouths open. In restaurants, people cracked ice with their teeth! But if I wanted to live here, I'd better get used to it, I told myself, and decided to make the best of it.

My first priority was to find a job as a photographer. This proved to be much more difficult than I had expected. No company wanted to hire a woman. They felt a woman needed a man to carry around her equipment, so the man might as well take the pictures himself. The only job I found was at the Waldorf Astoria on New Year's Eve.

Then came the tragedy. During the first week in January, Dr. Smith had a heart attack and died within a few hours. Besides shock, I felt a tremendous sense of loss. He was not only a very intelligent and caring person, he had been the only person in my new life who spoke German and who had helped me adjust to my new way of life. And, I cared very much about him. It was difficult to get through the funeral. The days following the funeral passed in a haze. Fortunately, his friends and relatives were very kind, and they invited me to their homes. Actually, I can recall very little about that time. It was so painful that I blocked everything out. I do not remember where I lived, what I did during the day, or where I ate, with the exception of a few visits with Dr. Smith's relatives and friends, who went out of their way to help me. Actually, it was the whole Jewish Hungarian community that helped me through this time and finally found a job for me.

As one of Dr. Smith's friends, I was invited to the home of a former minister of defense of the Hungarian People's Republic. He and his wife spoke some German, and she told me about their difficulties adjusting to a new life. Her husband had always been addressed as "His Excellency," and she was called "My Lady." Now, she shook her head sadly; he was called "Pop," and she was "My Dear," which by European standards is very demeaning. Europeans are very formal in their method of address, and one always used titles. I was learning fast. When people called me by my first name, I expected it and did not blink an eye. However, even now, when small children call me by my first name, I cringe.

CHAPTER 25

Through all this turmoil, my sponsor, Dr. Wright, was always in the background ready to help, and I will always be grateful to him.

The search for a job continued. Finally, I was accepted at the Modern School of Photography in New York as an instructor. Most of the students worked at the UN, which was located not far from the school. Most of them were also from foreign countries, so I fit right in. I taught the students many German darkroom techniques and was pleasantly surprised how welcome my instructions were. It was a pleasure to work at the school. Unfortunately, it was impossible to live on the salary.

When Dr. Smith's cousin told me of a jewelry wholesaler looking for help, I decided to go for an interview. I think I got the job before I was even questioned. Because they had previously employed a German girl who had been very efficient; the owners hoped I would be like her. When my prospective employer

100

asked about my mathematical knowledge, I had to admit defeat. Math had been my worst subject in school, and I thought I had no head for figures. They asked me if I would be willing to learn, and I readily agreed. The strange thing was that soon I was very adept at it and have been ever since. My first paycheck was for $50! Since I did not know anything about jewelry, other than that I loved it, and gold was gold and silver was silver, I had a lot to learn.

The first thing the girls I worked with did was to change my name to Sigi. Sigrid was much too difficult to pronounce, they declared. I have grown to like my nickname. Now, if somone calls me by my long name, at first I think I have done something wrong.

My first job in the factory was to match diamond and wedding rings. This was new to me. In Germany, our custom is different. When a couple becomes engaged, they wear their wedding rings on the left hand; and after the marriage, they switch the rings to their right hand.

Though in Germany I had studied English for eight years and taken a special class in conversational English, it was not easy to understand everybody in the factory. Desperately one day, I told one of the girls in the office that I could understand all the girls so well, but I could not make out what a young man in the factory was saying. They laughed and said, "Don't worry, we don't understand him either. He is from Puerto Rico and his English is very poor." What a relief!

After a few weeks in the factory, I was promoted to the diamond office. Now it began to get really interesting. The diamond buyer bought and sorted the lots or parcels that he had bought, then gave them to me to sieve into different sizes. This was done with special jewelers' sieves with inserts of different sizes. We started with the insert that had the largest holes first, then used smaller inserts, until all the stones were divided into different sizes. The end result would be many piles of stones. These diamonds would then be weighed and counted to find the average size (carat) of the stone. After this was accomplished, I distributed them into special envelopes according to the supplied instructions which listed the size and quantity of stones required for a certain piece of jewelry. The envelopes were then sent to the factory to be set. It was delicate work since some of the stones were so very tiny and could easily get lost or drop out of our tweezers. It happened to my boss once when he was looking at a large stone. It jumped out of his tweezers and disappeared through our eighth-floor window and was lost forever.

The owners and employees of this company were all Jewish. I was surprised and grateful for how well they treated me, a German girl. Mr. Besh, the owner, often asked me if I could get along on my small salary, and fussed about my high heels being too unhealthy. He was so genuinely concerned for my welfare that I was deeply touched. Never before and never after have I worked for someone like this.

Some of the diamond dealers who came to sell their goods appeared to be a little wary of me. My boss, Tim, explained that some had lost relatives in concentration camps, and he begged me to understand their behavior. I was glad they at least tolerated me. I felt sympathetic towards them and tried to be very quiet and, if possible, "invisible" around them.

Sometimes funny and embarrassing things happened to me because of my unfamiliarity with American English and its expressions. Since I was working with two men in a separate, secured office, I barely had any contact with the girls in the outer office, so I could not learn from them. Tim in particular had his fun with me. One time he sent me out and said I should order "Fatchalada Sauce" for lunch. He kept asking me how I liked it. I just grinned broadly at him. I was not that easily tricked.

After he heard how much trouble I had finding somewhere to go for lunch, he asked another young woman in the office, Josie, to show me how I could help myself at Horn and Hardart (a self-service restaurant, also called the Automat). The young woman was not very friendly and spoke only when asked. She showed me the Automat where a person could buy sandwiches. The sign outside the food display compartments told people how many nickels and dimes customers were required to put in the slots in order for the door to the food to open. Never having heard of dimes and nickels before, I assumed they were like subway tokens. I asked Josie how much each was worth and where I could buy them. When my turn came with the cashier, I asked for three dimes and a nickel, handing her three ten cent pieces and one five cent piece. The cashier gave me a disgusted look and shoved the coins back at me. There I stood, devastated and embarrassed! What had I done wrong? I looked at the coins in my hand and questioned my companion about it. Finally, she explained it to me. I did not dare tell Tim about it—he would have another laughing spell. He had already told me that I was quaint. But these were lessons you could not learn from school books.

Another time I got into an even more embarrassing situation. The plant foreman, who came frequently to our office, loved to be complimented. When he appeared with several other men, I noticed how he was trying to get attention with his new bow tie. Not knowing the English name for a bow tie, I was trying to be smart and translated it exactly from the German word for it and told him, "Harold, I sure like your fly." The result was stunned silence and red faces. Innocently I looked around and said, "What did I say now?" "Go to the other office and ask one of the girls for an explanation," Tim choked. After learning what I had said, at first I was mortified. Soon I shrugged it off thinking that they knew that I had no idea what I was saying; and I could not take it back anyhow.

It was interesting to work with diamonds and jewelry, and I loved it. Soon I was working overtime almost every day—sometimes until nine or ten at night. The extra money was welcome and gave me a chance to send more packages home to Germany. I hardly ever went anywhere in New York and needed very little for myself, but my habits would change.

CHAPTER 26

I lived in a rooming house on Long Island with a lovely Canadian couple, Mary and Dan. I rarely saw the other tenants and did not even know how many lived there. My next-door neighbor was an old lady originally from Germany. She seemed to be well off, but one day I was startled when I saw her coming from her room almost in rags. She must have seen the pity in my face or was embarrassed to be seen like this, for she explained that she was going to the dentist; and if she was dressed well, he would charge too much. I was very surprised at how little pride she had. It was completely un-German.

Most every night Mary and Dan called me to their living room to watch TV with them. It was a wonderful way to learn American English and an even better way to learn to understand it. For a while I just sat there and watched, not able to make out what they were saying, but it got better all the time. Lawrence Welk and Dinah Shore were my landlady's favorites, and soon I was singing with the rest of the world "Drive your Chevrolet through the USA," etc.

Gradually I learned American customs and manners, such as not to eat with the fork in the left hand and the knife in the right hand at the same time, and to keep your left hand under the table; to say "You are welcome" after somebody thanked you; to say "How are you?" and answering "Fine, thank you," when actually you were feeling rotten; and not to take it seriously when somebody told you to come and see them when they had no intention of following up on it. These are just examples. If you want to live in another country, you have to make up your mind to speak that country's language and adjust to the regional customs. (Later, relocating to the South proved to be another adjustment!)

Mary and Dan showed me a lot of the countryside. We drove to East Hampton and into the Catskills, along with other interesting places. What a lovely and generous couple they were, devoting so much of their time to my welfare. They really made me feel at home.

Several other girls stayed in the same rooming house, though I rarely saw thems. So it was a surprise when one of them, a girl from Holland, approached me and asked me to go to a party with her. Another girl from the house had invited us, and she would only go if I went along. Since coming to New York, I had never partied; work had been my whole life, so this was the last thing I wanted to do over the weekend. Who needed distractions? But, she insisted. The people giving the party needed more girls to have enough dance partners, and we would be really welcomed. Not wanting the other girl to miss out on it, I reluctantly agreed. But I made sure there was a subway close by so I could escape whenever I wanted.

When we arrived at the party, it was awkward at first. I did not know anybody, but I patiently waited for things to happen. And happen they did. A young man asked me to dance. Hank was a graduate from a well-known military college and, as an army officer, had been stationed in Germany during the Korean war.

It was past midnight when he and his friend took the Dutch girl and me home. From that day forward, we saw each other constantly. I met his roommates and the flight attendants who lived one floor above their apartment, with whom the boys had good relationships. We all frequently got together and shared many meals.

CHAPTER 27

Within three months of meeting Hank, we decided to get married.

When I met Hank, he had just resigned from his job to move back to Florida, where he had grown up. However, I was not ready to be unsettled again. I had just gotten used to New York. I enjoyed the occasional shopping in the German stores on 86th Street and being just a hop and a jump away from Germany. To leave would mean to sever all ties with my native country all over again, and I could not face it. My friends in the jewelry business described the South as being so poor that one should not be surprised to find outhouses in backyards. They thought this because our cheapest products were sold to the South. The move to Florida definitely needed to be more closely investigated.

So I set out, on the invitation of my in-laws, to visit them in Pensacola for a brief vacation alone. Was I in for a surprise! Blue skies, beautiful sunshine, green palm trees, and friendly people greeted me on my arrival.

My in-laws had a nice two-story house, two bathrooms instead of an outhouse, and even a washing machine. Was I going to enlighten them in New York! My time in Florida was so relaxing and enjoyable that I did not need any persuading to move there.

CHAPTER 28

Hank went first to get settled, and I followed by train. In Europe we travel a lot by train, and I wanted to have the American experience. How disappointing this proved to be. I could not see any cities, and what I could see were a lot of abandoned shacks and a vast countryside of fields and woods, barely any life. I got a good idea of how big and spread out this country is, and it overwhelmed me.

One particular person I remember was the conductor who started working on the train in Georgia. I could not understand a word he said. He examined the book I was reading, nodded in satisfaction, and said very slowly, "You studying English? You need it." He was right, though even today, I have trouble deciphering some of the Georgian dialect.

My lack of knowledge was pointed out to me even more, when I applied for a job and failed the written test that was given. How could I answer, when on most lines I did not even grasp the question? And I had never heard mathematical terms in English—you don't learn this in school. But in spite of all the testing going on in the business world, it did not take me long to find a job in the accounting department of a paper company. Since I was working in an office by myself, it was not easy to make friends. There was also no one my age; they were either much older or much younger. But they all were very nice to work with. A few years later, Hank was transferred to Tampa.

The same paper company I had worked for previously had a branch in Tampa and called me to worked for them as credit manager. I was still unfamiliar with how the credit system worked and had to learn from scratch. I got to know other credit managers over the phone, and we exchanged information frequently. Calling customers to pay their bills was no fun, and sometimes people were not so nice, but it was part of the job. I was really amused, though, when one day a customer whom I talked to a number of times over the phone showed up at the office to see me. Wondering what he wanted, he only grinned and said that he wanted to see if I looked like I sounded over the phone. He decided I did. Still today, my accent is very obvious, particularly over the telephone.

We started to settle down, and we built a house in the suburbs of Tampa. I had to learn how to drive, and Hank decided he would teach me. Out in the country he put me in the driver's seat and told me to drive. Since he is taller than I am, I had trouble reaching the gas pedal and sat in an uncomfortable position. Also, I could not see anything in the mirror since it was not adjusted for my height. Well, he knows best, I thought, and started driving. At one point, he told me to make a turn into a side street. Not having a sense of how much I needed to slow down, I screeched around the curve and landed right in front of a telephone pole. That did it! I continued the lessons with a professional driving instructor. And lo and behold, it did not take any time to learn the rules of the road, and soon I had my driver's license.

CHAPTER 29

After a while we felt settled enough to start a family, yet nothing happened. I had surgery after surgery for abdominal cysts, some with severe complications, but to no avail. Finally the doctors decided that I had enough surgery; and when they found that I had another cyst, they performed a hysterectomy. This shattered all our dreams of ever having a family. When I suggested adoption to Hank, he would not hear of it. I could not bear it anymore and decided to go on a long vacation to my parents in Germany. I would find comfort with my family and friends.

In New York (while en route to Germany), I went on an extensive shopping excursion and bought a number of gorgeous cocktail dresses. I decided to live it up and forget. A friend of mine from New York boarded the "Bremen," bound for Bremerhaven with me, and we enjoyed ourselves. Unfortunately, she became very seasick; and several days were lost for her. Nothing bothered me. One lady remarked that it was not ladylike to be so healthy, as almost everybody had a bout with it at some time. (With all my ailments today, I guess I have finally become a "lady.")

We attended most of the social functions on board ship; and in no time, we were surrounded by friends. One couple was from California, and the others were architects from different German cities who had attended a convention in the U.S. There must have been more than twice as many men as women, and I never lacked for dancing partners or someone to take me to the movies or other social events, of which there were many. Never before and never after have men stood in line to dance with me. My self-esteem was being restored, and I felt like I was coming out of a deep depression. Maybe I had some good points after all.

My parents were glad to have me back, and it gave me a chance to get to know my sister's children better. My father was an enthusiastic traveler and photographer. Immediately, he put me to work retouching his pictures. While looking at all the wonderful foreign places in his photos, I had an idea. With lots of time on my hands, why not take an extended trip and see more of the world myself? My father loved the idea, and together we made plans about what was worth seeing. We finally decided on a Mediterranean cruise. I visited Italy, Greece, Egypt, Turkey, Lebanon, and Cyprus. I was completely absorbed in not only studying the history of these countries but experiencing them as well. I never once gave a thought to my troubles.

CHAPTER 30

I vacationed for six months but then had to return to the U.S. During my long absence from Florida, I had a lot of space and time to think about my future.

Back in Tampa, I found a job as a secretary. But still I was not happy; so much was missing in my life. The terrors of the Nazis and WWII had left me with the strong desire to help others. I knew first-hand what it felt like to go hungry and do without any amenities in life. From this point on, my whole life became one of service to others. When I saw an ad in the newspaper that the American Red Cross was looking for volunteers, I knew this was what I wanted to do. After a short training period I was sent to a nursing home to assist another volunteer in taking care of the needs of the sick and infirm. Nurses did not have the time to look after the welfare of all the residents, so we were to relieve them of some of their burdens. Soon I learned how to communicate with them. I had a good teacher in the other Red Cross volunteer. She showed me that touch was very important, so I made it my routine to hug them a lot and, sometimes, press a kiss on their cheek. I helped them walk in the hallways, I fed them, and I listened to their problems. Soon I got familiar with their different needs and responded to them. When I walked down the hall, arms were stretched out to me, and some learned to call my name. One precious lady, who had been the nursing director of the largest hospital in the area, followed me everywhere with her eyes. After I found out how much she liked sweets, I made it a point to stop off at a bakery and get some doughnuts before visiting her. This went on for several years until the administration decided to terminate volunteer work in 1967, because we were not covered under their insurance policy, and they did not want to take any chances.

CHAPTER 31

A year later, in 1968, my father got sick with stomach cancer. Neither he nor my mother were told what he had, and he clung to life till he lost the battle. When I came to see him, he was so happy and immediately started making plans for trips. We were glad he never realized that he had a terminal illness and that he never gave up hope.

Again, I took the "Bremen" back to New York from Europe. This time I did not go for much socializing but spent most of my days on deck reading or in the swimming pool, exercising. Shortly before New York, reporters came on board and took pictures for the society pages in our home towns. My boss was very upset to discover my picture in the paper; he thought I should have flown back. I had such an easy job that sometimes I had to hunt up some work to look busy. I never thought it mattered when I came back, since I was not paid during my time away anyway.

My mother was in poor health and depressed for a long time, and Hank and I wanted to help her. Finally, she agreed to come and visit us for six months. She loved Florida and the American people, and her stay had a healing effect on her. When she returned to Germany, everybody thought she looked ten years younger.

In 1970, Hank finally suggested we adopt a baby. I had never mentioned it again, since I felt it was up to him now. We applied at an agency and succeeded. On October 30, 1970, we picked up our little son, whom we called Christopher Neal—Chris for short. He was three weeks old and soon became the joy and center of our lives. For the next 18 years, I would become involved in every phase of his life. From kindergarten through high school, I enlisted in volunteer work. I typed and graded papers, xeroxed tests, and taught photography at a prep school for one year. It was fun getting to know other parents, as well as teachers.

CHAPTER 32

An important part in our lives was knowing a wonderful elderly couple, "Grandma" and "Grandpa" as they were called by all. Before building our house, we had met them through our contractor. Grandpa was the one who drew up the plans for our house.

Both had lived in Argentina and Uruguay for many years, where Grandpa directed the Swift packaging plants. Many of their customs were English, and they adhered to them in the U.S. One of these customs was to have tea. So, almost every Sunday we were off to Grandma and Grandpa's house for tea. Grandma was a wonderful storyteller, and listening and talking to her made me feel relaxed and at home. They both passed on many years ago now, but they will always stay in my memory for being so warm and loving to all of us.

While Grandma was sick one day, I was introduced to Dr. Norton while visiting her. First I thought he was a physician making housecalls (though unheard of in this country, they still do it in Germany today). But he turned out to be the minister from her church. I liked him immediately. When Grandma asked us to go to church with them, we agreed. Her neighbor asked me to meet with the women's group of the church, the WOC, which had regular gatherings once a month. We liked the church, but meeting with the women made me feel very shy.

For some reason I had always been in awe of American women, thinking them much superior to me. They all had so much to say, and I sat quiet as a mouse, because I had nothing to contribute to their conversations. It all seemed so different, and I thought I never would fit in. This soon changed dramatically.

One day, while Chris was taking his nap, a woman from the church appeared on our doorstep wanting to talk to me. It was not so much a friendly visit as it was a business one. The WOC was in need of a new Christian Community Action chairperson, since she was taking a more important position. For some reason, they had decided I should be her successor. "I cannot do it" was my first thought, as it had been so many times through the years, but I had always managed to do it anyway. After assurances of guidance and help, I accepted.

In the beginning, I just listened to what was expected of the job, but then I decided to listen to the women express what their wishes were for the future. My motto has always been "never stand still, always grow and strive to improve situations. Be creative." This was the beginning of Sigi's rise through the ranks of church officialdom.

CHAPTER 33

Grandma had a good friend, Annie. Annie was very outspoken and fun, but often critical. One of her greatest wishes was to have an old-fashioned Christmas party. I told her, "You want it, you get it." This was the beginning of a long, 17-year line of such parties.

We started with sixty people, men and women over 65, and the last party had a participation of 120. The parties proved to be such a success that mothers, sisters, and friends of members asked to be invited also.

The Women of the Church, or sometimes the church cook, prepared a delicious warm meal free of charge. Our guests looked forward to the games, to Santa Claus (who gave them a hug and a gift), and to the caroling. In later years, we did a lot of pantomime, which let many people participate and created a lot of laughter.

To stuff Santa's stockings, we applied each year to a well-known cosmetics company for help. They were most generous and sent us beautiful as well as useful gifts, from their stock of discontinued items. We also applied to banks for pens, to stationery stores for little calendars, and to salesmen in our congregation for notebooks. Every year we sewed and decorated stockings. When the stockings became too small, we used paper bags and filled them with all the goodies we had collected. Santa talked and hugged everybody, so they were delighted with so much attention. All this would not have been possible without the assistance of some really super women, hard-working teenagers, and a talented young man who directed the singing and played the piano. He especially had a wonderful way to inspire everybody to sing along.

Words are inadequate to describe the warm, caring, loving fellowship we experienced. We were one happy family. My heart was full of joy and gratitude when it was over. To see and make other people happy has always been one of my goals. In German we say, "Und die Freude, die wir geben, kehrt ins eig'ne Herz zurueck" ("The joy we give to others will return manyfold into your own heart").

Besides Christmas parties, we had an annual Thanksgiving tea party. This was an elegant affair, where we displayed our best silver, linen, candles, flowers, and food. Other events happened seasonally and at random.

To do more in the area of group activities, I took classes in recreation, which were offered by the church. These classes gave me lots of inspiration. Books, too, were a good source of information. But experience is the best teacher, and I learned the likes and dislikes of our guests quickly.

CHAPTER 34

I served the Women of the Church faithfully and became more confident of my abilities. But not to the point of accepting the position of president of the Women of the Church. The current president told me she had consulted Dr. Norton, our minister, and he too thought me a good candidate. I was touched by their faith in me, but thought again "No, I cannot do it," and begged for time to think it over. I prayed a lot about it. One day I got the answer. I was standing in the kitchen, when I stopped in my tracks. An inner voice told me, "You can do it." So I figured, if God is on my side, I will not be a failure.

As most things in life, I approached my new task with a lot of energy and enthusiasm. You cannot accomplish anything in life without these two attributes. To put new life into this organization, I had to be innovative and find programs that appealed to women. Besides standard circles, we started an arts and crafts circle and a mission circle. Some ladies were interested in visiting a nursing home and bringing cheer to the afflicted. We inspected several to find where the need was greatest and found a black nursing home in a poor section of town. Several ladies took turns visiting each week and taking small birthday gifts from all of us to those who had added another year to their life.

Another thing I was very proud of was the little monthly newspaper we published. I was very fortunate to have found a good friend, Mary Ann, with a degree in journalism. She wrote beautifully. We called the paper the EVE-nts. Our logo was an apple with a bite taken out of it. A very talented lady provided the illustrations. Besides publishing all the ongoing events, we made room for an "Orchids and Onions" column; a "Mystery Lady," (where everybody had to guess who she was); and an "Out of the Mouth of Babes" column, (where everybody was invited to submit the cute sayings of their children or grandchildren). Mary Ann wrote a serious article, since we did not want to appear too frivolous. I had to struggle with the President's message, but was much more adept with the humorous part of the paper and really came up with some wild ideas. Together, we edited everything; and, voila, there were the EVE-nts. They seemed to be read and liked by everybody. The best compliment I heard was when one man announced that when he got his mail and saw the EVE-nts, he dropped everything and read them first. We carried on with the paper through two other presidents of the Women of the Church.

CHAPTER 35

During my last year as President of the Women, I was also elected to serve on the Session (church council) as an Elder, which I am today. I did a lot of soul-searching. So much had happened in my life, yet I was saved during critical encounters and disasters. I could see God's hand in everything and felt tremendously grateful. For all I received, I needed to give something back in return; and I made an even greater effort to serve and help people to the best of my ability. In all this, I was inspired by our minister, who had so much confidence in me. If it had not been for him, I never would have dared to speak in front of hundreds of people. He supported me in every program I introduced.

As chairperson of the membership care committee, my responsibilities increased manifold. The elderly were of great concern to me; they were so lonely. We started going on bus trips to the Lake Wales Passion Play, Cypress Gardens, Silver Springs, and other places. I made sure they were entertained on the way with lots of singing, even if it meant taking the microphone and leading the singing, by myself or with the help of a friend. Our voices were not very good, and I did not know some of the American oldies, but nobody was too shy to join in, and we had a lot of fun.

Chris had to come along on all of these excursions, and the elderly really loved to have a small child around. He kept writing little love letters and distributing them to whomever he took a fancy to. Once when we had to stop on the road because our bus had broken down, he picked wildflowers on the side of the road and handed them out. To me it was a way of keeping him busy. He also helped me set up for parties, for which there seemed no end by this time. Just recently someone told me that when they think of me, they think of a "colorful party girl."

My telephone was constantly busy. Knowing that I loved and cared for the elderly, they called me all the time, and it was difficult for me to hang up on them. A solution was needed for this. I made a list of those calling the most and decided to match them up between themselves, thus our telephone friends were created. Did they ever love it! Most of them called each other every day, talked for hours and became good friends, though they hardly ever saw each other. They were so concerned about each other that they called me when their partner would not answer the phone.

It was part of my job to organize retreats. We had, among others, a program telling us about God's love and named the retreat a "Love-In." Others were called "Pray-In" and "All in the Family." Our minister took care of the speakers; the rest of the program was up to me and my committee. Fortunately, everybody chipped in and helped. No one can ever do everything alone; it is teamwork. Those were wonderful times—canoeing down the river, falling in the water when the canoe tipped over, swimming, square dancing, sitting around the campfire, playing all kinds of ball games, and hiking through the woods. The children had their own fun times, and normally teenagers took care of them. And the food was delicious and plentiful and tasted even better after we were outdoors all day. What a time we had!

CHAPTER 36

1981 was a very crucial year for me that changed my life forever.

Our minister, Dr. Norton, decided to retire, and arrangements were made for interim pastors, as well as a steering committee, to continue the life of the church. Then plans for the retirement party had to be made. He had been with us for so long and had been instrumental in building the church, as well as building up a large congregation, everyone agreed something very special needed to be done. We formed a committee to organize the party, and I was a member of it. Everybody was assigned a certain task, but the bulk of it stayed with me. What else is a party girl to do?

We had several guest speakers from around town, a men's quartet, and a big dinner in the garden of the church. To honor Dr. Norton's wife, who was the sweetest person anybody would want to meet, I read a long poem that I had written about her accomplishments. Then I handed her a cap and gown and gave her a degree from the Hope Presbyterian Church School of Human Relations. In the beginning, I was not quite sure how this would be received, but when one of her sons mentioned how fitting this was, I was happy. It was a memorable affair on which I think back proudly.

Since I was an Elder and a committee chairperson, I was elected to be on the steering committee. To my horror, they elected me chairperson. It probably was not so much because of my knowledge as my ability to deal with people that got me that position. Somebody made the remark I was always so full of enthusiasm that it was infectious. It was an awesome responsibility. But I was not alone and got a lot of help from the church's financial secretary, as well as the secretary and an interim minister. We also had an exchange pastor from England, whose church Dr. Norton had taken over for a few weeks. Serious misunderstandings occurred in our church, and it worried me deeply. With the help from our interim pastor, we approached Presbytery for advice. I breathed a sigh of relief when they told us that officially, Dr. Norton was still our pastor; and we were to contact him.

I finally got in touch with him in England and explained the situation. He said right out that we had reason to be alarmed, and we were not to go through with the plans the English pastor had made for us. At all costs, we were to stop him. The longer we talked, the more upset I got, and I felt a headache coming on. It was so excruciating that I was unable to talk and said a hurried good-bye, not giving any reason.

I called Chris to bring me some aspirin but was not able to swallow it. All of a sudden I started vomiting; I had lost control of myself. My nephew was visiting from Germany, and I begged both of them to call the ambulance. They were quick in coming; however, they thought me a drug addict, because they saw the white aspirin pills still lying on the bed. When they asked me to turn over in bed so they could put me on the stretcher, I lost consciousness and did not regain it until three weeks later.

I had a cerebral hemorrhage and cardiac arrest. Due to my heart problems, brain surgery had to be postponed. During my coma, I was aware of two incidents. One was a friend from church feeding me soft food; and another, our minister whispering in my ear that I should not worry anymore, everything was fine. The next memory came when the nurse shook me. The neurosurgeon was there to check me over, and I saw two strange men standing in front of my bed. One of them smiled and said to the nurse, "She will be all right now; she does not need surgery. What she needs is a TV to stimulate her brain." I do not remember their leaving, since I was in "Neverland" again.

Soon after that I became more aware of my surroundings and wondered about all the machines around me. The nurse laughed; this was only a small leftover of what I had been hooked up to. I should have seen it before!

Another short memory is of my sister standing there with her son and my husband, Hank, but I do not remember if they said anything or when they left. When I finally came out of it, I felt a real sense of loss. I had been floating, and everything was so peaceful and happy; it was an awful shock to be back in the real world. I wanted to drift back so badly!

After they transferred me to another room, I still had one problem after another. I was concerned about the effect it had on Chris, since he was only ten years old. I asked my doctor if he could visit me. The first time Chris saw me, he rushed to my bed and wrapped his arms tightly around my waist, as if he did not want to let me go; it made tears come to my eyes.

After five weeks of hospitalization, I was finally allowed to go home. But I did not want to go home; I felt secure in the hospital. I was afraid of any emergency that might arise when out of reach of doctors and nurses. They told me my chances of survival had been very slim. That is why Hank had been advised to call my family, and my sister had come. Mutti (Mother) did not know anything about it; she was told I had broken an arm.

It took me six months to recuperate. Everybody tells me it was a miracle, and I know God watched over me. I also had excellent physicians. I will always be grateful.

While I was still recuperating, I was informed of all the developments of the pastoral search committee, of which I was still a member. When the new minister came for an interview, I was able to meet him and thought he suited our needs.

Christmas was just around the corner. What about the party for the elderly? Nobody else was going to do it, so I decided I could organize a lot from home (since I was not allowed to drive for months). We had a wonderful party, even though I had to direct everything from a chair. My dear friend, Mary Ann, was a true trooper and watched that I did not overdo, and she did a lot of the physical work. All they really needed were ideas, of which I always had plenty.

The list of all those friends and people who helped me during this time is long, and I was very touched by this outpouring of love.

CHAPTER 37

My last achievement as an Elder was the forming of a singles group. I had been approached by a friend, who shared with me her discomfort of attending the theater alone or eating by herself at a restaurant. It can be a lonely life for anyone who has lost a spouse through death or divorce. I was enthusiastic about forming a group for single men and women that would help create companionship with each other and offered all my help to get approval from the session. After overcoming a few obstacles, they approved it. The group grew fast, and today they still have wonderful fellowship with each other. My biggest reward came, when a widow told me that the group had given her her life back. She died soon after, and it made me feel good to think that we could make her last years happy ones.

CHAPTER 38

Mr. Schiller, a retired German pastor, entered my life through Dr. Norton, my former minister. Mr. Schiller spoke only German and needed a translator. How could I refuse anybody in need? He did not only need somebody to speak for him, he needed to be looked after and cared for in many other ways. I visited him often and had him at our house on many occasions. Mostly I took him to various doctors, since his health was not good. Most of all, he needed attention since he was very lonely. Many times Chris had to go with me when I drove him around. On one such occasion Mr. Schiller kissed my hand as they did in "Old Europe." I did not think anything of it and thought Chris had not even noticed. However, as soon as we came home, he rushed to find his daddy. "Daddy, Daddy," he shouted, "Mr. Schiller kissed my mama!" He was so upset.

Mr. Schiller spent his summers in Germany and came back for the winter months to stay in Florida as long as he was feeling well enough to keep this pace. In 1988, a year before he died, I visited Mr. Schiller in his hometown in Germany. The small town had no access by train, so I had to take a taxi from the closest city. On my arrival, the driver took me to the only hotel in town. I was told that no rooms were available. Seeing my predicament, the owner told me with importance that they were expecting an American lady; if she did not show up, I could have her room. He was startled when I told him that I was the American. It seems my German heritage is still very much with me.

CHAPTER 39

When our beloved Grandma died, we "inherited" her friend, Annie. She always had been invited to have holiday meals with Grandma and Grandpa. After they were both gone, she had nowhere to go, so we felt we needed to do something for her. Never did we realize how much we would get involved in her life. She was a spry old lady, sharp as a tack, very wise, but also cantankerous at times. I cured her of the last trait by not visiting her for a couple of weeks after one of her outbursts, and she was the sweetest lady after that. She was full of jokes, and I marveled at her memory. I caught on to her, though, when I saw her studying her notes and memorizing the jokes just before going out to meet people. Her favorite one was that she lived with four men. She got up with Will Power, spent the morning with Charlie Horse, the afternoon with Arthur Ritis and went to bed with Ben Gay.

When she became ill and had to go to the nursing home I thought, "now her family can take over." But they called me. The grandson had told them to call Sigi; "She takes care of everything." So I did. Hank took care of her finances, while I looked after her well-being. For three years, we visited her every Sunday and cheered her up. She always introduced us as her children, and we almost felt like them. I started having birthday parties for her when she was still living by herself and continued that practice when she was in the home.

Annie lived to be 99 years old. In her mind, she was 100 and told everybody so.

CHAPTER 40

While Chris was still in high school, I was planning another trip to Germany. I sat at the kitchen counter looking at catalogs to bring me up to date on fashions. All of a sudden, I woke up on the floor. I had fainted, and the barstool had tipped over. Not being able to get up, I crawled to a telephone and called 911. Help came immediately, and I was rushed to the emergency room. My heart rate was up to 160, and in the ambulance on the way, the technicians tried all kinds of medications to get it down, but nothing helped. When we got there, they were waiting for us. The clothes were cut from my chest and electric shock administered. It was so loud, I thought the building would crash down on me. But I could breathe better, and my cloudy vision was restored. What a miracle it was! I was diagnosed with ventricular tachycardia. The medication I received for it helped only for a little while; and within a month, I had another attack, which again required electric shock. Now I was put on the strongest medication available to help prevent further attacks. It has worked for ten years now, and I feel confident that my problems are over.

All this did not keep me from continuing my volunteer work. After a brief pause, I started driving for Meals on Wheels again. These lonely people are so anxious for somebody to come and take an interest in them. We encouraged them to lead a healthy life, consoled them when they were sick, admired their scars, and brought a breath of fresh air into their lives. Sometimes a person on the route died or had to go into a nursing home, and we would miss them. But we tried not to get too emotionally attached to them; otherwise, we would worry too much. Unfortunately, this Meals on Wheels experience ended on a very sad note when they silently dropped me from their roster without explanation. I can only assume that they did it because I had been sick too much.

Having experienced all I have, I feel fortunate to be able to help others. There are so many needs around us, like the mother of three on welfare (along with her brother and sister-in-law) that my friends and I surprised with a carload full of toys, food, and clothes at Christmas delivered by Santa.

Then there was the German woman expecting her ninth child whom I found crying in her mother-in-law's backyard. The mother-in-law lived in filth, and she had nowhere else to go. How can we ignore such pain? The purpose of writing this is to open others' eyes, not only to the needs of others, but also the possibilities of what a person can accomplish if only they try.

CHAPTER 41

Being born and raised in East Germany, it was only natural that I kept up with the development in that country.

While I was still attending school in Dessau, the Communists started their own youth organization. From the age of six to ten they were called the Young Pioneers; from 11 to 14 they became the Thaelmann Pioneers (named after a Communist). My cousin assures me that it was a very loose organization which did not have regular meetings. The most noticeable difference from the Hitler Youth was how they greeted each other. The "Heil Hitler" was replaced by "Friendship." In school, teachers greeted the students with "Seid bereit" ("be prepared"), and students answered "Immer bereit" ("always prepared"). The FDJ, as this movement was called, had their own parades and sports festivals. They also wore uniforms. Everything was much like the Hitler Youth, though nobody would have dared to mention this similarity. Like the Hitler Youth, their main purpose was to indoctrinate the youth into the Communist ideology.

During my last school years in Dessau, we always hoped that the Americans would come back and free us from Communism. How could they have left us in the first place, we wondered? This gave rise to a lot of speculation. Bets were made as to when this liberation would occur. Friends knew from reliable sources dates when the Americans would come. Dates came and went and nothing happened. Gradually, all hope faded away. We were doomed. Many East Germans escaped to West Germany, until gradually all roads were blocked, no way to freedom existed, and the Berlin Wall was built. Occasionally we heard of heroic escapes, but mostly people suffered quietly. The East German "People's Army," the "People's Police," and the "Stasi" kept everybody under control; and people submitted to their force.

But the population got restless nonetheless. They saw what was happening in the world and became upset because they realized that they were left behind and enjoyed little freedom. Freedom of speech and freedom to travel which is so vital to other nations were nonexistent, and they wanted it badly.

During the 1980's, prayer meetings for peace started in the Nikolai Church in Leipzig. A young congregation from Leipzig East was instrumental in continuing this prayer chain for freedom week after week. A firm date was set for each Monday at 5 PM. Gradually, East Germans heard of these meetings and poured into the Nikolai Church, so many that the 2000 seats could not accommodate all the people. A school friend of mine faithfully went to these gatherings and told me how impressive it was—a unity in spirit. Never before had people formed such a tight bond as at this time. It was a wonderful feeling. She also told me "Reunification" was far from their minds, originally. They just wanted better living conditions, less pollution, free speech and the chance to travel to any country they wished to visit.

People prayed in church, lit candles, and walked peacefully into the square calling "Wir sind das Volk" ("We are the people"). Often the police waited outside for them. They beat up the demonstrators and loaded them into police vans to imprison them. The Nikolai Church became a shrine for the victims of Communism. The windows had iron bars, and the people put bunches of flowers in them as a memorial.

In the fall of 1989, the demonstrations started up seriously. On September 4 of that year, 1200 people demonstrated under the motto, "Freedom to travel instead of mass defections." There was no reaction from the police at this time.

On October 7, 1989, the DDR (East Germany) celebrated its 40th anniversary; today, this date is remembered in German history as a day of mourning. In almost all the big cities, including Berlin, Dresden, and Leipzig, the 40th anniversary celebration turned into a sad affair. With sticks and teargas, the police attacked those who demonstrated. Thousands were forced to flee the water cannons.

Appeals were published in the newspapers to stop the counterrevolution, because the government would use, if necessary, weapons to control the masses.

After all, Egon Krentz, the second-in-command under Erich Honneker, had approved of the Tiananmen Square massacre. What would stop him now?

Those were the conditions as the fateful October 9, 1989, approached. A gruesome force of military, police, and civil servants surrounded the demonstrators in the Karl Marx Square. For ten hours, uniformed communists beat up helpless and peaceful people and transported them in trucks to prisons. As I was told by my friend, the attackers had orders to shoot. It is to the credit of the Mayor of Leipzig and Kurt Masur, the conductor of the famous Gewandhaus orchestra, that nothing happened. They appealed to the young men that, in all probability, they would shoot against their own relatives. They appealed to their conscience, and the soldiers listened. One by one they withdrew. They had come so close to a massacre!

November 9, 1989, the Communist dictatorship was finally and peacefully removed. Another school friend wrote to me about how she had sat glued to the television watching how the Communist flags were being removed from government buildings. She had to pinch herself to believe this was really true.

CHAPTER 42

The opening of the borders and the removal of the Berlin Wall paved the way for our first high-school class reunion since our graduation in 1948. It all started with our Berliners. They set the wheels in motion to find out the addresses of several classmates in the hope that they in turn would be in touch with others. On June 9, 1990, we had our first reunion. I remember entering the waiting area of the subway in Berlin-Wannsee, scanning every woman to see if I recognized anyone. I saw several women grouped together, and I knew I had found them. By that time, they had discovered me, too. We looked each other over carefully to know exactly who was who. In 40 years, everybody changes and not only physically. Gradually, I discovered resemblances and certain traits that we had when we were young. We behaved like teenagers, talking nonstop. When we stopped for lunch at a restaurant, we were reprimanded for being so loud. For us it was such a joyous occasion, we thought only about ourselves. The first day was spent mostly hiking through the woods.

The second day, a large group of us took the train to Dessau. "Home sweet home" came to mind arriving there. But home was not so sweet anymore. I barely recognized the city and had trouble finding my way around. It was the first time in 40 years that I had set foot in my hometown. Marianne, my old school friend, and I went out on our own to find the houses where we had lived. Almost all the houses we found were in terrible shape. Ruins from World War II were still standing untouched; most buildings were sadly lacking a paint job and looked run down. Only certain houses where tourists came to visit were in excellent shape, like our old school, the Bauhaus. While walking through the city, we were surprised by a heavy rainstorm. One friend had walked under a gutter to find some protection only to be shocked with a regular waterfall on her head. The gutter of the roof had broken and unleashed the water over her head. She did not seem too surprised since she lived in the East; and, evidently, something like this was not uncommon. Are we in the West ever spoiled!

All my school friends drove back to Berlin the same night; however, I drove with another friend, Rena, to Leipzig, where I spent the night at her apartment. Being an American citizen, my visa stipulated that I had to spend at least one night in East Germany, and they really checked it out when I passed the border. Even in July, 1990, they still checked the borders.

While in Leipzig, Rena showed me around the city. We visited the Nikolai Church, which was of great interest to me. I wanted to see with my own eyes where the revolution started. We also went through the stores, where everything was on sale since the merchants were expecting shipments from Western countries. My batteries on my microcassette recorder had given out, so I wanted to buy new ones. When I showed the salesperson what I wanted, he sadly told me that they had only some batteries produced in East Germany, and they would not hold up very long. "How bad could it be?" I told myself. It was BAAAD! The batteries did not even last through one single tape!

While in the city, we decided to go out for lunch. After we found a nice restaurant, we had to wait in line outside for our turn. Upon entering the place, we saw that only half of the room was seated with people, the other side being completely empty and dark. We could not get a table by ourselves but had to share one with two men. After I questioned why the other side was not being served, the men told me that they did not have enough personnel to keep it open. When I questioned why all the many unemployed men and women in the city could not do that job, they looked at me as if I came from outer space. "But they need to be properly trained, and that takes years to fill such a job!" I told Rena, "Any teenager in the U.S. can do something like this." While we were still studying our menus, the lights went off, and we were sitting in the dark. They did take our orders but did not bring us a candle. Only after our meal arrived did we have the privilege of light! When we left the restaurant, a sign had been put up that said "Closed." A passerby told us that the same thing had happened the day before. No other blackouts had occurred in the neighborhood. Since the restaurant was still government-owned, nobody seemed to care.

This reunion brought our class closer together than we ever were before. We were all more mature and have come to treasure friendships more. Also, our families have grown up, and we have more time to devote to friends. We feel it is a gift that we have found each other again.

CHAPTER 43

Before I conclude this book, I need to tell you about my latest endeavor. At a banquet three years ago, I met a lady who was playing puppets with her church group, and she invited me just to watch them sometime. I was duly impressed by their skills and the impact it had on the children in different hospitals. One little boy was sitting next to me, grabbing my arm when it got exciting and chuckling gleefully about the whole play. Such a joy! In another hospital, children were clinging to their parents with frightened faces; and when they saw the puppets, they wiggled out of their parents' arms and sat down on little chairs of their own. Their faces lit up with a radiant smile, and they forgot all about the hospital atmosphere. Right then and there I decided that I wanted to have a part in making them happy. I am now in my fourth year working with the Puppet Show; the group has been in existence for ten years. It is under the direction of a professional puppeteer and ventriloquist who teaches us something new all the time. I still have a lot to learn. I may never be perfect; but if I give my best, it will be good enough.

Nowadays, I am also working with a retired professor from a local university to form a new puppet group at our home church. We both have enough enthusiasm to get other people interested, and I have no doubt that we shall succeed. So many organizations approach us to play for them that I know we will have many places to go to bring joy to others.

Think of all that is in store for us!

Class reunion in Berlin - Wannsee

As a Puppeteer with Mr. Clown

Church Christmas Parties

EPILOGUE

I am sitting at the beach on an island in the Gulf of Mexico. Peace and calm surround me. Barely a human being is in sight. I sit and watch the pelicans and seagulls flying by and marvel at their grace. Sandpipers are chasing the waves and are being chased by them in return. I laugh at their antics.

Not a ship is on the horizon. It sets me in a melancholy mood. The horizon reminds me of eternity. It is an eternity we live in. Generations come and go. They live with their joys, sorrows, and dreams. Sometimes the pain seems unbearable, but they hold onto life, which is a precious gift from God. And sometimes the joys make up for the hurts. I sit and think back on a life that was and could have been.

My thoughts also go back to the three years that have passed since I finished this book. They were eventful years!

For three years now I have lived by myself in a small house on a lake, and I am content. Sometimes I long for things that I will never have. But in this I am not alone. No one promised us that life would be easy; what matters is how we meet the challenges and to do the best we can according to our abilities. Fortunately, I have a good imagination and always find worthwhile things to do.

Five days a week, I do volunteer work. There is so much need around us, and it breaks my heart to see people suffering. Therefore, I go to a nursing home regularly and visit the sick, the lonely, and the poor. It is heartwarming to see how they thrive under my care, how their eyes light up when they see me, and how they miss me when I am on vacation. Last time I was gone, one lady walked the halls looking for me, murmuring "Where is she? Will she ever come back to us?"

I listen to their problems and encourage them to talk about their past lives. Those who have trouble concentrating I treat to stories that I partly make up. Sometimes I take one of my big puppets with me and let them talk to my friends. Some of the residents honestly think the puppets are real and talk to them in a baby language. The other day somebody asked me if my girl could already walk, and I told her that she was too small yet. They thought I should have a romance with my boy puppet, but then decided he was a little too small for me. I hug them a lot because touch is so important, and they whisper to me how much they love me. They are my friends, and I thrive on their love and wonder how I could ask for more in life?

I still work with puppets in local hospitals—my seventh year now. To see children in pain and in tears and being able to make them happy moves me deeply. They are so brave, and I admire their spirits.

I have taken to writing and rewriting puppet plays. It is often difficult to find scripts that we can use for our purposes. Sometimes it is a problem to find puppets to fit into the story. Instead of running around to find something to fit our need, I have decided to make it myself. I have never done anything like it. Three Japanese princes are sitting in front of me right now that I have designed and made from scratch. We all have so many more talents than we think we do, and everybody should try to find their potential.

A school invites me regularly to come and talk to the students about Germany and the Nazi period. I was surprised by their conception of what Germans are like. One student wrote to me, mentioning that he was surprised to find out that Germans are not all monsters of the Holocaust. All of the horror happened fifty years ago, and no one can compare the Germans of today with those living during that time. And even then it was only a certain group that committed those crimes, and the general population did not want to have anything to do with them. I am glad our youth is searching for the truth and is interested in a time they cannot even remember.

Last year, while I was in Germany, my mother became the victim of a flu epidemic. It was a shock to all of us when she did not wake up one morning. Though we know she is at peace, we miss her sorely. Life will never be the same without her loving presence. And now my sister and I have moved up the ladder to be the next to leave this world.

Chris continues to be the joy of my life. He is happily married and doing well in his job as manager in a computer-software company. He is still working to finish his master's degree in political science. (Writing his thesis is taking him forever.)

I still travel to Germany as much as I can and recently returned from a trip to

Mallorca, Spain, where my youngest niece from Hamburg got married.

Unfortunately, my health is not very good. I had two back surgeries and have trouble walking long distances like I am used to. My heartfunction is only 20%, and my doctors and other people wonder that I have so much energy—more than most healthy people, I am told. Nothing can keep me down, certainly no physical problems. And with a positive attitude, I can accomplish a lot.

In 1996, I finished another book, Party Time. It is for the mature adult and shares my many years of experience entertaining the elderly. It took awhile to compile this material, and I hope it will be a help to many who entertain large groups.

I have told you much of what has happened in my life, the shadow years and the light years. I appreciate your coming along with me on my Crossroads to Freedom.

CHRONOLOGY

1919	Treaty of Versailles
1933	January 30, Field Marshall Paul von Hindenburg, President of Germany appoints Hitler Chancellor of Germany
1936	Rhineland becomes remilitarized
1938	Austria is annexed
1938	November 9, Crystal Night
1939	September 1, Hitler invades Poland (Blitzkrieg) World War II starts
1940	May 10, German troops seize France
1941	June 22, Germany starts war with Soviet Union
1941	December 11, United States enters the war
1944	July 20, German officers try to assassinate Hitler at the Wolfsschanze (the Army headquarters)
1945	March 7, American troops cross the Rhine river
1945	Late April, American troops arrive at the Harz mountains and occupy the castle where we lived
1945	April 30, Hitler and Eva Braun commit suicide
1945	May 7, World War II ends
1945	July 1, Russian troops take over part of East Germany (the castle too) in exchange for part of Berlin which the Allies divide into sectors
1949	Germany becomes two different countries, the Federal Republic of Germany (West) and the German Democratic Republic (East or DDR)
1989	Revolution succeeds in East Germany
1990	October 30, both Germanys are reunited

PHOTO ACKNOWLEDGEMENTS

Kurt Lehmann (Sigi's father)- childhood pictures
Museum Ballenstedt - Castle Ballenstedt Aerial view and view
from the West
Sigrid Stoesen - Castle Ballenstedt-Church and Theater
Foto Loeffler, Altena/Westfalen - castle or fortress Altena
Sigrid Stoesen - Youthhostel and courtyard
Juergen Butter, Letteschule-Berlin - portrait as a young girl
Herr Kramer, Berlin - Class reunion
Nurse at University Community Hospital - as puppeteer
Putzger, Historischer Weltatlas, 102. Auflage, @1992,
Cornelsen Verlag, Berlin, S. 113 (bzw.122), maps of Germany
Village Photographers, portrait of Sigrid 1998